THE LAKE

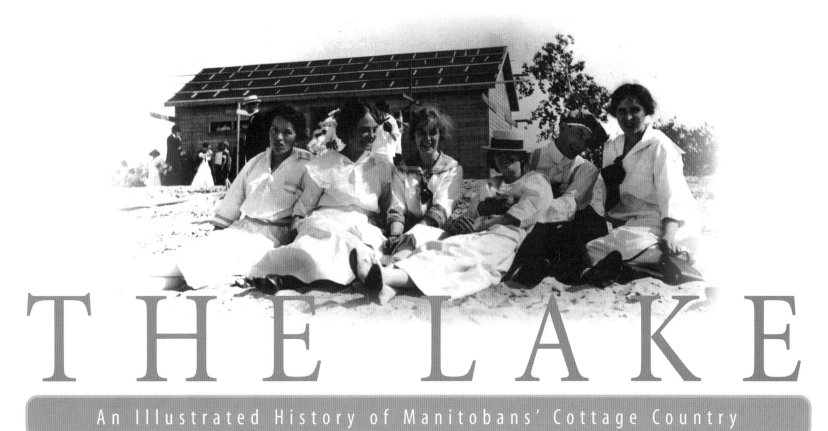

THE LAKE

An Illustrated History of Manitobans' Cottage Country

PHOTOGRAPHS BY TOM THOMSON & DAVE REEDE

EDITED BY JAKE MACDONALD

GREAT PLAINS
PUBLICATIONS

Great Plains Publications
3–161 Stafford Street
Winnipeg, MB R3M 2W9
www.greatplains.mb.ca

Great Plains Publications gratefully acknowledges the financial support provided for its
publishing program by the Government of Canada through the Book Publishing Industry
Development Program (BPIDP); the Canada Council for the Arts; the Manitoba
Department of Culture, Heritage and Citizenship; and the Manitoba Arts Council.

Design & Typography by Gallant Design
Printed in Canada by Friesens

CANADIAN CATALOGUING IN PUBLICATION DATA
Main entry under title:
The lake : an illustrated history of Manitobans' cottage country
ISBN 1-894283-12-0

1.   Lakes—Manitoba—Recreational use—History—Pictorial works.
2.   Manitoba—History, Local—Pictorial works.
3.   Manitoba—Social life and customs—Pictorial works.
4.   Outdoor recreation—Manitoba—History—Pictorial works.
I. MacDonald, Jake, 1949-

FC3362.L36 2000   971.27'009692   C00-920219-6
F1062.L36 2000

Rest is not idleness, and to lie sometimes on the grass on a summer day listening to the murmur of water, or watching the clouds float across the sky, is hardly a waste of time.

— Sir John Lubbock

PREFACE

BY JAKE MACDONALD

As I sit at my desk and look out the window, I see a blustery afternoon with yellow leaves gusting by. It's an odd time of the year, perhaps, to be launching a book about "the lake." But this book is a valuable form of displacement activity. Last fall, about this same time, a Manitoba publisher gathered together a group of writers and photographers and said: "Well, you can't be at the lake, but at least you can write about it."

The publisher was Gregg Shilliday. A former journalist, Shilliday runs Great Plains Publications. Coincidentally, Shilliday expressed an interest to me a few years ago about returning to the lake country. He'd been living in Alberta, and missed the glint of sunlight on blue water. He wanted to wet a line, hear a loon, hoist an Irish whiskey, toast his feet by the fire, and do all the other things that people do at the lake. I was heading down to Minaki for my end-of-season chores, and invited him along.

I like going to the lake in the late autumn. It's a somber time of the year, when the lake is black, bitterly cold, and the bays are boarded over with ice. Shilliday was a good helper, and we spent the day shutting things down at my summer place. Afterwards, we went out and caught some walleyes

for dinner. Chilled to the bone, we docked the boat, piled wood into the old CNR stove and enjoyed a hot meal of walleye fillets, baked potatoes, and fried mushrooms.

Shilliday was so invigorated by his trip to the lake that he bought a boat the following spring, and has been a regular visitor to Minaki ever since. Shilliday's attraction to the lake is informed by gusto and a love of the outdoors. But the attraction is different for every Manitoban. For some, a cottage at the lake offers the opportunity to relax and sunbathe after a long house-bound winter. Some see it as a refuge, a place to get away from phones and meetings. Others look for the opposite — a place where the socializing never ends. As one teenage girl told me last summer, "I've got this whole end of Lake of the Woods hard-wired for fun."

In fact there are probably as many reasons to go to the lake as there are lakes themselves. And the evidence comes every Friday night, when thousands of Manitobans hit the highway to visit a campground, lodge or beach. Lakeshore real estate is affordable in this part of the country and another 12,000 Manitobans own cottages — which is the highest per capita level of cottage ownership in Canada.

In this book, a collective of Manitoba's best writers and photographers attempts to answer the question of why we go to the lake in their own unique and impressionistic manner. Some writers, like myself, spend much of the summer at the lake. Others, like Charles Gordon, travel long distances to enjoy a brief respite from big city life. Some, like Christopher Dafoe, travel distances of memory as they recall lake experiences from the past. But most of the writers featured in this book are probably like you — leaving work early on Friday to head out from the city for a weekend of escape.

With so many perspectives on the lake experience, there's no authoritative or correct way to organize this sort of collection. So we treated it much as we would a party at the cottage. We compiled a list, invited some lake-dwelling writers, and trusted in the belief that they would entertain us with their nostalgic, comic and touching tales of life at the lake. If their stories share anything in common, it's not so much a theme as a point of view. "I like my house in the city," these writers say, "But I love my place at the lake." ■

LIST OF CONTRIBUTORS

DOUGLAS ALLEN

Based in Winnipeg, Douglas Allen's sporadic forays into the field of journalism have included contributions to the *Manitoba 125* history series and *Cottager* magazine.

INGEBORG BOYENS

Journalist and author Ingeborg Boyens currently works as a producer with CBC's *Country Canada*. Her book, *Unnatural Harvest*, won the National Business Book Award.

MARTHA BROOKS

Martha Brooks is a fiction writer, playwright and jazz singer. Her latest book *Being with Henry* won the McNally Robinson Book for Young People Award and the Mr. Christie's Book Award.

C. J. CONWAY

A former Ontarian, C.J. Conway is a Vancouver-based writer who owns a cottage on the Lake of the Woods. His latest book is *The Lake of the Woods*.

CHRISTOPHER DAFOE

Editor and journalist Christopher Dafoe has written several books including *Winnipeg: Heart of the Continent* and the comic novel *The Molsheim Meadowlark*.

CHARLES GORDON

Author of several best-selling books, former Manitoban Charles Gordon writes columns for both the *Ottawa Citizen* and *Macleans* magazine.

DAWN GOSS

Writer/photographer Dawn Goss lives and works from a one room schoolhouse near Erickson, Manitoba. Her work has appeared in *Time*, *Equinox*, *Canadian Geographic* and *Cottage Life*. She is the recipient of two national magazine awards.

BRIAN JOHNSEN

A Winnipeg freelance writer, Brian Johnsen has spent much of his life cottaging in the Whiteshell.

JANIS JOHNSON

Senator Janis Johnson has fly-fished for Atlantic salmon in Newfoundland and sailed in the Adriatic. Her favourite place in the world is Gimli.

ALLAN LEVINE

An educator and author, Allan Levine's most recent book is *Sins of the Suffragette*, a sequel to his best-selling mystery novel *The Blood Libel*.

JAKE MACDONALD

Proud owner of a refurbished Peterborough boat, Jake MacDonald is a Winnipeg-based writer who spends his summers in Minaki. His latest novel is *Juliana and the Medicine Fish*.

MARY JANE MACLENNAN

Currently teaching at Red River College, Mary Jane MacLennan is a writer and broadcaster who has lived all across Canada, but "likes Winnipeg the best." She has a cottage on Big Whiteshell Lake.

ELLEN PETERSON

During the week, Ellen Peterson is a theatre artist and freelance writer. The rest of the time she can be found at her cottage two hours east of Winnipeg with Rob, Carly and her big red dog.

CAROL PRESTON

Former managing editor of *The Beaver* history magazine, Carol Preston is now much in demand as a researcher for both book and film projects.

BILL REDEKOP

An award-winning journalist with the *Winnipeg Free Press,* Bill Redekop has contributed to several books including the best-selling *A Red Sea Rising*.

DAVE REEDE

A professional stock photographer, Dave Reede specializes in documenting the natural beauty of Manitoba's lake country.

STEVEN SCHIPPER

When not golfing, Steven Schipper acts as artistic director of the Manitoba Theatre Centre. He is married with two children.

JIM SHILLIDAY

After working for many years as an editor for Winnipeg newspapers, Jim Shilliday is now enjoying a so-called retirement writing books — including a biography of Saskatchewan's "Wheat King" Seager Wheeler.

TOM THOMSON

Born and raised in the Lake of the Woods area, Tom Thomson developed an interest in photography and photojournalism. Tom still resides in the Lake of the Woods area with his wife and three children.

DUNCAN THORNTON

Despite occasional intervals of camping and farm-work, Duncan Thornton's soft city hands show he makes a living by writing, teaching, and developing interactive media products. His most recent book is *Kalifax*.

GENE WALZ

Prof. Walz is the author of several books, including *Cartoon Charlie: The Life and Art of Animation Pioneer Charles Thorson*. He teaches film studies at the University of Manitoba.

ON MANITOBA'S
INLAND
SEAS

The Lake Winnipeg/ Lake Manitoba Region

BY CHRISTOPHER DAFOE

It is one of those clear, warm, windless prairie mornings in the early summer of 1911. My grandparents in their Sunday best take the CPR train north from Winnipeg to get their first look at Ponemah Beach, named for "the land of the hereafter," in Longfellow's *Hiawatha*. They alight at the small community of Matlock near the south end of Lake Winnipeg and, turning their faces once more to the north, begin to walk along the shore, around large rocks and through cool thickets of willow.

THERE ARE A FEW COTTAGES here along the low bank above the shallow lake, simple wooden boxes with steep roofs and screened verandahs, but for much of the hazy space between where they stand and the distant green blur of Dunnottar Point, three miles away as the gull flies, the shoreline is thick with trees. My grandmother names them: poplars and cottonwoods, mostly, but with a few large and ancient oaks and a dim green and yellow border of marsh willow. The shore is littered with broken stones and strewn with large, smooth boulders, with occasional lengths of brown sand crinkled by the passage of the waves. Shells — small and white, large and pink — crackle under their feet. The far side of the lake is a thin line on the horizon. What the eye can see, vast as it is, is only the small lower basin of an immense lake that forms part of a water system, lakes and rivers, that bisects the province. It is more like a sea than a lake and is, in fact, the remaining puddle of what was once a huge inland sea in prehistoric times, a relic of the Ice Age. Lake Winnipeg is not tidal, but it ebbs and flows nonetheless, as if governed by the great moon that appears over it on summer nights.

The sun pours down and I think I can see my grandfather, a trifle warm in his suit, his necktie snug about his neck, stopping from time to time to mop his brow. My grandmother fans herself with a straw hat and talks of lemonade. Gulls soar and dive above them.

A Dafoe family picnic, circa 1906.

In the still, moist woods above the shore — where cottages will grow in profusion in years to come — hundreds of birds feed on insects and sing and shout: Baltimore orioles, woodpeckers, catbirds, waxwings, bad-tempered kingbirds, yellow warblers, crows and hummingbirds, their loud music vying with the steady drone of waves on the lake. Along the shore, sandpipers and terns skip and hop. A chipmunk, great great great great grandfather to the chipmunk who will one day take peanuts from my young hand, capers along the bank.

Far down the shore, almost at the Point, over a short length of sand and up a slight bank, my father's parents find what they have been looking for. The cottage — green and white with a verandah around three sides and a small flagpole on the point of the roof — is theirs for the summer, with an option to buy.

My grandfather admires the tall oaks and catches a glimpse of white birch deeper in the wood. My practical grandmother notes the lack of a well and the presence of an outdoor biffy and speculates on the amount of coal oil needed to illuminate the cottage interior at night.

As a result of the building of the CPR line from Winnipeg to Winnipeg Beach, a series of resort villages like Ponemah soon developed on the west shore.

At the front door of the cottage they turn and admire the view. Lake Winnipeg seems to go on forever. The far shore, 20 miles away, is like a broken line in a child's drawing. The lake gleams and sparkles in the sunlight. Whitecaps roll over the rocks and surge up the beach, foaming. A slight breeze makes the poplars tremble.

"We'll try it for a summer," says my grandmother.

15

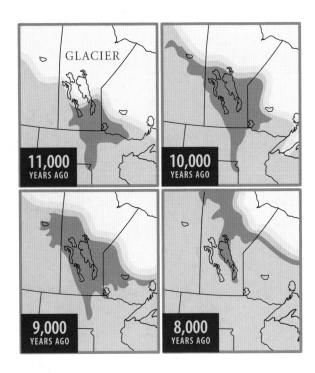

11,000 YEARS AGO

10,000 YEARS AGO

9,000 YEARS AGO

8,000 YEARS AGO

GLACIER

The precursor to Manitoba's big lakes was the prehistoric Lake Agassiz which was created by retreating glaciers during the Ice Age.

IN THE MIND OF A CHILD, Time Past and Time Present can exist in the same magical space. When my brothers and I were children playing on the shore of Lake Winnipeg not far from my grandparents' cottage, we sometimes imagined that we could see York boats and Indian canoes far out on the lake, bringing supplies and trading goods down from York Factory to Red River. At certain moments we were sure that we heard the rhythmic chanting of the Métis rowers above the roar of the waves and the shouting of the gulls. On warm summer nights as we sat around a bonfire on the beach watching the sparks fly up toward the stars, we were voyageurs ourselves, resting on the shore by our overturned boats and heaped bales of fur and pemmican after a hard day on the lake. Camping on the shore, we dreamed of Indians arriving for the first time in their canoes, nomads from the east and north looking for new homes, new hunting grounds. Time stopped and made the dream seem a reality. In the embers of our campfire we saw history, alive and kicking.

Far back in time the big lakes of Manitoba were part of one great inland ocean, the vast glacial Lake Agassiz, the largest of the many Pleistocene lakes of North America, which once covered vast stretches of Manitoba and the surrounding plains. Over the ages the one great lake shrank and became many, returning as a mere shadow of itself in great floods over the centuries. Now, viewed from the air, Manitoba offers a pattern of lakes, great and small, with three dominating the map: the enormous Lake Winnipeg with its two great basins, cousin to the Great Lakes of the East; marshy, shallow Lake Manitoba, and, above it, the crook-shaped Lake Winnipegosis, fed, in places, by salt springs.

The big lakes of Manitoba were highways over the long centuries, trade routes for Indians and incoming Europeans, with brigades of canoes and York Boats moving briskly along, followed by fleets of fishing boats from Gimli and steamboats of the Hudson's Bay Company from Norway House and beyond. Great schools of fish — pickerel, whitefish, catfish and armoured sturgeon as large as canoes — swam in the sandy but nonetheless pristine waters; clouds of birds followed the lakes on their annual migrations, resting in the many marshes and in woods along the shores; herds of bison wandered the woods and plains; insects buzzed and hummed in the swamps; battalions of frogs sang in the summer sunshine; squadrons of dragonflies drifted in the clear air over the lakes. Storms shifted rocks and sand along the shallow lake bottoms, creating long beaches, sandbars and dunes. A thousand winters, and as many summers, springs and autumns, shaped the shorelines after the glaciers melted away.

Numerous Aboriginal groups passed this way over the centuries, camping along the shore, making homes, giving names to geographic features, telling stories and creating legends about the spirits, gods and magic places of the countryside. When Peguis and his Ojibway people crossed the lake and pitched camp close to Netley Creek near the end of the eighteenth century, they were only the latest in a long procession of wanderers to find a home, permanent or temporary, among the Manitoba lakes.

Henry Kelsey of the Hudson's Bay Company may have been the first European to see the great lakes of Manitoba in the 1690s when he travelled south with the Cree, who called them "win-nipi"

(murky waters), a name adapted later for the largest of the three and the sixth largest in Canada. Winnipegosis, the eleventh largest lake in Canada, was named by the Cree "little murky water." La Vérendrye saw Lake Manitoba in the 1730s, calling it Lac des Prairies. The Cree used the name "manitobau" or "place of the spirit" because of the magic they found near the narrows in Canada's thirteenth largest lake. Cedar Lake, above Lake Winnipegosis and almost touching the upper basin of Lake Winnipeg, makes a fourth "great lake."

Henry Youle Hind, who visited Lake Manitoba on an expedition in the 1850s, encountered the magic of the past when he landed on "Manitobah Island" in the lake that gave its name, in slightly altered form, to the future province. It was a place of great and potent magic, avoided by local travellers out of respect, but Hind and his companions set up camp and spent the night. They heard strange sounds, like the singing of spirits on Prospero's enchanted island. "These sounds," he wrote later, "frequently resemble the ringing of distant church bells; so close, indeed, is this resemblance, that several times during the

The York boat was the backbone of the Hudson's Bay Company's freight delivery system, transporting supplies back and forth from southern collection points to company factories in the north.

A rare image of a giant raft carrying timber on Lake Manitoba, circa 1891.

PAM, N12767

Icelanders escaping both economic and physical calamities in their home country settled on the west shore of Lake Winnipeg near present-day Gimli.

night I woke with the impression that I was listening to chimes. When the breeze subsided, and the waves played gently on the beach, a low wailing sound would be heard from our camping place, about 300 yards from the cliff where the noise was produced." The Europeans had a simple explanation for the wailing: waves were calmly breaking over the smooth rocks at the base of the cliff and entering small caves, producing a sound like distant bells and singing, unremarkable to the prosaic visitors, an enchantment to the imaginative natives.

On the same expedition Hind noted that lakes were already being used as places of recreation by European settlers, especially a small lake between the lower ends of Lakes Winnipeg and Manitoba, not far from present-day Woodlands. "Shoal Lake," he wrote, "is a favourite sporting ground of the gentlemen of Fort Garry and the half-breeds of the settlement." In the years to come, recreational hunting would also find its way to the marshes of Lakes Winnipeg, Manitoba and Winnipegosis. The observant Hind also noted the "tidal" effect on the Manitoba Great Lakes, a hindrance to travellers since boats were first used in the area and to campers and cottagers in the years ahead: "Canoes left in calm weather on a beach high and dry are not infrequently washed away when a strong south or north wind sets in…"

In the 1870s Icelandic immigrants settled along the shore near Gimli and on what had been known as Big Island, called by the Icelanders "Mikley" and, later, "Hecla." The Icelanders and other settlers who gradually moved into the land between the lakes did not initially see their new homes as a place for recreation. There was too much hard work to do. They were there to establish new homes in an often hostile and unforgiving land and, for the Icelanders especially, the early years would be extremely hard, with starvation and illness frequent visitors and no time for play.

By the 1890s, however, Winnipeggers were increasingly looking to the Manitoba "great lakes" as possible holiday resorts, although they remained difficult to reach. Manitoba hunters from Brandon, Portage, Winnipeg and other towns were attracted to the marshes of Lakes Winnipeg and Manitoba for autumn duck hunting and many established lodges and shooting boxes along the shore.

Two pioneers of summer camping on Lake Winnipeg were Miss Sarah Miledge, a "Lady Matron" at St. John's College, and her friend Miss Talbot, who spent part of the summer of 1892 roughing it in a tent at Gull Harbour on Hecla Island, arriving there by steamboat from Selkirk after a 12-hour journey. The ladies were so pleased with their experience that they recommended Gull Harbour to several of the professors at the College and in 1896 Miss Miledge and three clerics, Canon S.P. Matheson (who married Miss Talbot), Canon G.F. Coombes and the Reverend C.R. Littler purchased 660 feet of frontage at the bottom of the

Although this photograph, taken near the Delta on Lake Manitoba, may appear to show people staring at trees rather than the lake, it is more likely another photographer was shooting his friends with the lake as a backdrop.

PAM, Delta 3

From Bathing Machines to Bikinis

BY CAROL PRESTON

The first recorded use of bathing costumes was in Greece around 350 B.C., when women wore togas for public bathing. Later, as a mosaic wall from a fourth century Sicilian villa shows, young women wore scanty garments resembling the modern-day bikini. After the fall of the Roman Empire, use of water for recreation went out of style for more than a thousand years.

In the eighteenth and nineteenth centuries, "bathing machines" were used by most women to sea-bathe in privacy. As this horse-drawn cabin-on-wheels was pulled into the sea, the bather changed into a long flannel smock, and a matron, or "dipper" lowered her into the water.

During the same period, nude bathing was the norm for men. When the moral climate finally restricted this practice around 1880, men switched from birthday suits to the "University Costume," a striped, short-sleeved garment worn at Cambridge since 1517. The Eaton's catalogue for 1901 offered a "men's combination bathing suit, navy ground, with fancy cardinal and white stripes around neck, arms, and legs." Although men's swimsuits closely resembled their undergarments, they were not allowed to "go topless" on American beaches until 1937.

Cold-water dunking eventually led to the recreational use of beaches by all classes for swimming, diving, and sunbathing. Such activities required — especially for women — a special costume that combined modesty with freedom of

This 1893 picture shows a girl who is clearly unhappy with the neck to ankle coverage of her bathing costume.

Until the 1930s, both men and women had to maintain decorum at the beach by keeping their tops covered.

movement, but there was no precedent except the toga. Gowns proved a disappointment (except perhaps to male observers) since they floated up in the waves. Into the 1890s, the bathing attire of most women still consisted of cumbersome dresses and corsets, which weighed about ten kilograms when wet.

Fortunately for women, North American swimwear underwent a revolution in 1907 when swimmer Annette Kellerman introduced the snug-fitting, black-wool, one-piece suit that became the dominant look in swimwear into the 1920s. But, from this point, swimsuit design diverged along two tracks: the functional and the fashionable. In 1908 the *Brandon Sun* reported that a beach-time feature was a new bathing suit of satin foulard, "satin-surfaced materials much the smartest just now, are matched by shoes, cap and parasol in very stunning effect."

During the evolution of the swimsuit in the twentieth century every change in design, which usually resulted in the exposure of more skin, was met with opposition from the guardians of morality, but the tide of public opinion eventually won out, with the help of swimsuit manufacturers and their close allies in Hollywood.

The "flapper" era of the 1920s led to the acceptance of the basic tube-shaped swimsuit for women, and the 1930s brought backless and sleeveless suits for tanning, which was then all the rage. The post-war was marked by a return to glamour and an emphasis on the bust (in swimsuits of new synthetic fibres developed during the war for military use). The 1950s saw the transformation of the swimsuit into a decorative garment designed more for social use than for swimming. It was also the decade when Vancouver seamstress Rose Marie Reid, became the success story of the 1950s with her "constructed" suits designed to minimize figure flaws.

In the 1960s the baby-boomers reached young adulthood, and embraced the bikini and beach culture, which was celebrated in music and in movies like *How to Stuff a Wild Bikini*. The bikini had been introduced in France in 1946, but was rejected by North Americans at that time as too risqué. In 1964 Rudi Gernreich presented his topless suit, but it never really caught on, perhaps because it was more erotic to leave something to the imagination.

By the 1990s suits were made of lighter fabrics, were less structured, and cut high at the sides. Such suits reflected the new emphasis on working out (to wear them required "tight and toned" bodies). Many Manitoba women were happy to wear the new suits at summer hotspots like Grand Beach, which led *Playboy* magazine to call it "one of the top ten beaches in North America." ■

bay. Cottages were erected and soon a small summer community, with views of Deer and Black Islands, and inhabited largely by Anglican clergymen and their families, sprang up, flourishing well into the twentieth century, a remote and peaceful retreat.

Winnipeggers' love affair with Lake Winnipeg really began in the first year of the new century. In the hot summer of 1901 Sir William Whyte, a Canadian Pacific Railway official, cruised along the western shore in a hired motorlaunch, scouting for a site on which to establish a summer resort. A short distance up the lower basin, near what was then the northern boundary of Manitoba, he found exactly what he wanted. He saw over the waves a three-kilometre crescent of sandy shoreline with poplar woods and marshy fields beyond. Frogs croaked and mosquitoes hummed, dragonflies hovered in the deep blue sky and the waves of Lake Winnipeg rolled up the shore and landed with a roar on the brown sand. Sir William turned to his companions. "This is the place," he said.

Winnipeg was growing and the citizens of the "new Chicago" needed a place out of town where

This very early photograph (circa 1908) shows one of the first trains arriving at Winnipeg Beach.

PAM, Winnipeg Beach 21

they could recreate themselves after the long winter and escape the smells and noises of the city during the short, hot summers.

Wealthy Winnipeggers had already discovered the pleasures afforded by island retreats at Lake of the Woods. By 1901, however, the CPR was ready to help less well-off Winnipeggers to a place in the sun, and incidentally do a bit of business at the same time.

Sir William set the project in motion. A few miles of lakefront were purchased, a hotel and a dance hall were put up and the CPR began to lay a rail line over 40 miles and more of bush and swamp. The tracks reached the townsite in 1903 and Winnipeg Beach began its summer years.

Over the next few years the resort flourished. Cottages went up at Winnipeg Beach and along the shore to the south and north. Two hotels did a brisk business. An amusement park with a ferris wheel, roller-coaster and other attractions drew large crowds.

The first motor car reached the beach in 1913, badly damaged after a long journey over rough trails. A proper road of sorts went through in 1915, but it was still a long trip, with frequent

PAM, Foote 1217

Rowing competitions were a favourite pastime of daytrippers at Winnipeg Beach in 1912.

stops to repair punctured tires. Most people still came by rail and would continue to do so for years to come. The fare in the early days was 50 cents and that included free dancing at the Pavilion. The railway was extended to Gimli in 1906 and to Riverton in 1914.

Matlock, Whytewold, Ponemah, Winnipeg Beach, Boundary Park, Sandy Hook: the railways made the Lake Winnipeg resorts possible and, for a generation or more it dominated them. Only a brave few used the highway in the early days and trains were needed to carry huge crowds of Winnipeggers out to the beach on summer weekends that began after offices and shops closed at noon on Saturday. Dances in the Pavilion, one of the largest in western Canada, attracted large crowds through the twenties, thirties and forties, and hundreds came out for picnics and outings on Saturday afternoons. On one warm Sunday in 1920 the CPR had 13 trains on the line. There were regular trains every day in the summer until the automobile triumphed in the 1950s and for almost 50 years there were many "specials" on the weekends.

PAM, Ransom, Edgar J. Collection 398

⬤ This picture will no doubt end up in the cottage hall of fame as one of the few images ever depicting men washing up after a picnic.

"Fresh Air" camps for Winnipeg children, usually sponsored by religious groups, Roman Catholic, Protestant and Jewish, were established along the western shore and gave many Winnipeggers their first taste of beach life. Unions also sponsored camps.

The early success of Winnipeg Beach and other CPR-sponsored resorts on the west side of Lake Winnipeg prompted MacKenzie and Mann's Canadian Northern Railway to look at the east side of the lake with the intention of developing rival attractions. Shortly before the First World War the railway acquired a fine shoreline property adjacent to Grand Marais (Great Marsh), a place visited and named by La Vérendrye in 1738. The property, containing a magnificent sandy beach two and a half miles long and a lagoon, was named "Grand Beach." A rail line from Winnipeg was completed in 1916. Tenting sites were made available for campers and soon cottage lots were offered. By 1920 a hotel and sports facilities had been built.

With the collapse of the Canadian Northern, the resort and rail line were taken over by the

Even though fashion styles dictated being covered from head to foot in the early 1900s, these daytrippers at Grand Beach seem to be enjoying themselves nonetheless.

The Hunting Lodges
of Lake Manitoba

BY JAKE MACDONALD

PAM, Foote Collection 321

● Whether it was royal protocol or just good luck, the Prince of Wales, later Edward VIII, outshot his companions during a visit to the Delta Marsh in 1919 by bagging 82 ducks.

The east side of Lake Winnipeg is Shield country — with long shorelines of exposed granite — and its sandy beaches are simply rock that's been pounded into powder by wave action. The other big lake in the province, Lake Manitoba, doesn't have much in the way of exposed rock, so its beaches tend to be muddier, with a shallower gradient. Most cottagers therefore settle on Lake Winnipeg. But if you ask any mallard duck where he'd rather spend his holidays, Lake Manitoba would be at the top of his list. Muddy shorelines and shallow waters make for great marshes. And the Delta Marsh, at the south end of the Lake, was once the greatest waterfowl gathering place in North America.

Since the construction of the Fairford Dam on the west side of the lake, stabilized water levels have destroyed much of the Delta Marsh. But in the glory years before the dam was built, wealthy sportsmen, Hollywood movie stars, and European royalty travelled to the Delta Marsh, stayed at local lodges, and hunted with the Ducharmes, Lamirandes, Lavallees, and other Métis families who lived alongside the lake. Most of the Lake Manitoba Métis trace their ancestry back to the buffalo hunters who helped feed the giant fur trade enterprises of the early nineteenth century. They've always been hunters, fishermen, and trappers, and they settled on Lake Manitoba because it is rich in wildlife. When the lake began to develop a reputation as a hunter's paradise, back in the early 1900s, the Métis took the opportunity to employ their skills as outfitters and guides.

In the autumn of 1901, a flag-draped Royal Train arrived at Lake Manitoba. Governor General Lord Minto, Prime Minister Wilfrid Laurier, and the Duke of York (later King George V) had travelled all the way from Ottawa to visit the Delta Marsh. With local Métis guides (none of whom were identified in existing photographs) the Royal party canoed into the marsh and spent three days shooting ducks over hand-carved wooden decoys. According to newspaper accounts of the time, the Duke bagged 82 ducks — far more than anyone else in the party. But who would dispute a bird that fell within a quarter-mile of a future monarch?

Edward the Prince of Wales must have heard his father talk about the fabulous shooting because he paid his own visit to the Delta Marsh in 1919. The Prince first completed a tour of western Canada, where his every movement and gesture were lavishly depicted in the newspapers. But the same newspapers played dumb on his hunting trip to the Marsh, and described it only as "several days rest in and about Winnipeg." Some photographs were taken of the hunt. And this time, the sponsors were egalitarian enough to identify John, Alex, Moses, and Baptiste Lavallee as the guides to the Royal shooting party. A few years later, Edward met Mrs. Simpson and evidently lost his enthusiasm for the great outdoors.

In 1935, famous American trapshooter, magazine writer, and *bon vivant* Jimmy Robinson built a camp called "Sports Afield Lodge" at the Delta and hired the Lavallees, Ducharmes, and other locals to work as his guides. In those days, there was a kind of cross-

● Hollywood legend Clark Gable (centre), along with friends and Métis guides, shows off the results of his hunting prowess during a 1940 visit to Lake Manitoba.

pollinating effect between the shooting sports and the Hollywood movie industry. Teen-age trapshooting champions like Robert Stack were spotted by talent scouts and offered careers in film. And some of the reigning film stars of the day became noted competition shooters. Fred McMurray, Don Ameche, Ginger Rogers, Howard Hughes, Gary Cooper and his red-headed wife Rocky (one of the best shotgunners in the United States) hobnobbed with Jimmy Robinson at the Santa Monica Gun Club during the 1930s, and Robinson invited most of them to come duck hunting in Manitoba.

One afternoon in 1940 the girls behind the counter at Cadham's Hardware in Portage La Prairie did a double-take when a handsome mustachioed gent in a beat-up leather jacket arrived to buy a hunting license and a couple of boxes of shells. Their hearts beat even faster when they looked at the name that he signed on his hunting license — "Clark Gable". It was only one week since they'd wrapped up the shooting for *Gone with the Wind*, and Gable was looking for some fresh air and a well-deserved vacation. Gable was one of those no-

nonsense Hollywood stars who very much considered himself a friend of the working classes. And during his one-week stay at Robinson's lodge he cleaned ducks, played poker with the guides, and helped Edna, Shirley, Margaret, and the other Métis ladies with the dishes. Jimmy Robinson described Gable this way: "He's strong as a bull, six feet one inch tall, weighs 200 pounds, is fast as a cat, and is an exceptionally fine duck shot." Frank Lavallee, Gable's elderly guide — who was himself famous for having never uttered a swear word in his life — had even higher praise for Gable. "He's a real gentleman."

In the last few years, Ducks Unlimited and other conservation agencies have had some success restoring the health of Lake Manitoba's marshes. With the help of complex dike systems, powerful water pumps, and large infusions of donated money, small portions of the marsh are gradually being nursed back to life. It may be many decades, however, before Lake Manitoba once again regains its status as one of the greatest waterfowl gathering places in North America. ▄

Canadian National Railway and the development of Grand Beach as a rival to Winnipeg Beach began. A huge dance hall, said to be the largest in Canada, was constructed. There was a boardwalk with rides, like the one across the lake. The first hot dog stand went up in 1923. On the large picnic ground 1200 could be seated at once. A small cottage community developed in the vicinity, the earliest temporary dwellings, called "Donaldas" and made of wood and canvas, supplied by the railway.

Winnipeggers and other Manitobans flocked to the new resort. The *Free Press* had its first staff picnic there as early as 1916. An annual Caterer's Picnic brought thousands to the resort. On the July long weekend in 1920 almost 500 would-be passengers had to be turned away because there were not enough rail cars to carry them. About 8,000 people managed to make the journey that weekend. Like the CPR across the lake, the CNR had its own "Moonlight Special" to bring crowds to the dance hall on Saturday nights and home again at midnight.

Cottage communities sprang up along the eastern shore at Patricia Beach, Hillside, Balsam Bay, Grand Marais and Albert Beach, which for

GRAND BEACH

FINEST BATHING BEACH IN THE WEST

CANADIAN NORTHERN

MOONLIGHT DAILY 5.20 P.M. 50c

Saturday, August 5th

12.00 Noon (SPECIAL TRAIN) 1.05 p.m., 5.20 p.m.

The Excursion Special returning will leave Grand Beach at 7.30 p.m.

SATURDAY 1.05 AND VICTORIA BEACH MOONLIGHT TRAINS TO

WEEK-END ACCOMMODATION—Week-end Fare, $1.75. Meals and first-class sleeping accommodation, Saturday p.m. to Monday a.m., $4.50 additional. Go any train Saturday, return Monday.

BATHING -- DANCING -- FISHING -- PICNIC FACILITIES UNEXCELLED.

CANADIAN NORTHERN

STANDARD TIME SHOWN ABOVE

Call or phone F. J. Creighton, City Ticket Agent, Canadian Northern Railway, cor. Portage Ave. and Main St. Phone Main 1066.

CANADIAN NORTHERN

many years attracted French-speaking vacationers. By the late 1920s it was possible to travel to Grand Beach by car, but the railways held their own until the years after the Second World War. While Grand Beach and Winnipeg Beach cheerfully catered to Manitobans from all walks of life, Victoria Beach, located a few miles north of Grand Beach, was founded to provide a more exclusive, sedate and tranquil retreat for those wishing to avoid dance halls and the hurly-burly of the boardwalk.

The exclusive resort was established by a consortium of Winnipeg investors on a sandy peninsula, the first lots going on sale in 1911. The resort could only be reached by water at first, but in 1916 business arrangements were made with the Canadian Northern, which extended its line. The arrangement also involved the railway in a new Victoria Beach Company, which had close control over the development of the resort. Strict building standards were established, the removal of trees was controlled, amusement rides were not allowed and "day-trippers" were discouraged. Victoria Beach was to be a "family resort." Motor traffic was also banned within the community, cars eventually being left in a parking lot on the edge of the townsite.

There were no written rules about who could or could not own or rent a cottage there, but it was generally assumed that Victoria Beach catered to a largely Anglo-Saxon group drawn from the middle class of Winnipeg.

The question was aired publicly in 1943 when a Jewish family expressed interest in purchasing a cottage. The *Victoria Beach Herald* newspaper was quick to respond in an editorial: "Remember, you have an obligation to see to it that those unwanted people who have over-run beaches on the other side of Lake Winnipeg are not permitted to buy or rent here." In what may have been an attempt to appear helpful, the *Herald* pointed out that "We do not cater to them here. We have no means of supplying them with special foods or meat." The *Free Press*, on the other hand, saw the *Herald*'s editorial as a simple piece of Anti-Semitism worthy of Dr. Goebbels, describing it as "a sanctimonious and cowardly piece of Jew-baiting."

Cottagers on the other side of the lake may have felt smug, but the fact remained that few, if any, Jews could be found inhabiting cottages at Matlock, Whytewold or Ponemah in those days. In fact, as late as the 1960s a few residents were still objecting to the prospect of having Jewish neighbours at the beach. All were welcome at Winnipeg Beach and Grand Beach, however, and many Jewish families from Winnipeg enjoyed summer holidays at cottages at Boundary Park, Sandy Hook, Gimli and Loni Beach. The past was not always as perfect as memory suggests.

Cottage life and memories of life at the beach are remarkably similar, no matter what side of the lake you remember best and what part of the twentieth century you are thinking about. The same sun and rain fell on both sides of Lake Winnipeg and they fell, in turn, on cottagers at Delta Beach and Twin Beaches on Lake Manitoba and along the sandy shores of Lake Winnipegosis. For children it was a life in the open air, two months without shoes or intense supervision, a season of bonfires and mosquito bites, with the distant sound of arriving and departing trains like a siren call through the summer trees.

PAM

● Unlike the railway-sponsored resorts of Winnipeg Beach and Grand Beach, Victoria Beach was developed by a consortium of middle-class Winnipeggers who wanted to avoid the raucous crowds of the other towns.

● Inset: A typically tranquil Victoria Beach cottage.

Knishes and Chips at Winnipeg Beach

BY ALLAN LEVINE

Meeting the train at the Winnipeg Beach station, 1915.

PAM, Winnipeg Beach 35

If you were young, Jewish, a resident of Winnipeg's North End in the 1940s and 1950s, and it was a Saturday night in the summer, there was only one place to be. At about five in the afternoon, you would have hopped a streetcar headed for the CPR Station at Higgins Avenue and Main Street. Crowds of teenagers already would have been there, milling around the nearby Royal Alexandra Hotel.

"There were always lots of kid waiting," recalls Freda Morry, who moved into the city from her home in Holland, Manitoba when she was a teenager in the late 1940s. "We knew everyone and three-quarters of the kids were Jewish."

At 6:30 p.m. everyone boarded the CPR's "Moonlight" train for the 70-minute ride to the town of Winnipeg Beach. The fare cost 75 cents for a return trip. The Jewish teenagers were a well-behaved bunch. "There were no problems with liquor in those days," claims Allan Chisvin, now a Winnipeg chartered accountant. But Chisvin does remember that the train did have sleeping cars attached to it and the boys — sometimes without success — attempted to spend the ride to the Beach snuggling and "necking" with their girlfriends.

When they finally arrived at their destination, usually the first stop was a visit to Kelly's cabins and food stand for the finest "chips" money could buy. After that there was a leisurely stroll on the Beach's famous Boardwalk by the lake, where the object was "just to be seen." The Boardwalk's main attraction

was an amusement park owned and operated by Harry Silverberg, a prominent Winnipeg Jewish community leader and businessman. Winnipeg Beach boasted one of the great roller-coaster rides in western Canada sure to generate loud screams in addition to the popular bumping cars and games of chance ("toss the ball") in which you could win a box of chocolates or a stuffed animal.

For the teens, however, the highlight of the evening was the Beach's Dance Pavilion, a mammoth barn-like structure that was later converted into a roller-skating rink. In the years after the Second World War, the Dance Hall featured live bands and some of the best musicians on the circuit.

Today, five decades later, their time at Winnipeg Beach remains a warm and powerful memory. The Beach offered just the right mix of fun and excitement. "It was," Freda Morry says, "a magical time. That's the best way I can describe it."

The Jewish love affair with Winnipeg Beach began almost the moment the CPR executive William Whyte established the resort in 1903. The Beach was close to the city and accessible by an inexpensive train fare. The CPR station was also on the edge of the North End, where the majority of Winnipeg's Jews lived, and reached easily by streetcar. But most importantly, the Beach was one of the few lake resorts in Manitoba where Jews were welcome.

At more fashionable Victoria Beach on the other side of Lake Winnipeg, for example, there was a

widely accepted gentlemen's agreement not to sell property to Jews — a rule that had been applied rigorously since at least 1914. Victoria Beach's White Anglo-Saxon summer residents did not even want Jews to visit the area. In the summer of 1943, a Winnipeg Jew managed to purchase a cottage at Victoria Beach setting off a storm of protest. In an editorial entitled, "Unwanted People: A Reminder to Property Owners and Rental Agents," the *Victoria Beach Herald* told residents that, "You have an obligation to your neighbours at Victoria Beach. Remember you have an obligation to see to it that those unwanted people who have overrun beaches on the other side of Lake Winnipeg are not permitted to buy or rent here…If these people are allowed the run of the beach, it would soon degenerate into a Coney Island…We do not cater to them here. We have no means of supplying them with special foods and meat…We have an obligation to those who have zealously guarded Victoria Beach. Let us keep the kind of resort for which it is famous by doing everything in our power to keep out The Unwanted."

While the *Winnipeg Free Press* denounced the *Herald*'s article, comparing it to what was then transpiring in Nazi Germany, the majority of Winnipeg Jews were more than content to stick with Winnipeg Beach. Since most of them could not afford to buy their own cottages, the Jewish boarding-cottage was invented. Enterprising families purchased large cottages and rented out small areas by the day or week. While the husbands remained in the city to work during the week, their wives ran the boarding cottages. Ziporah Torchinsky operated a place in the 1920s and Dina Fogelman's cottage on Spruce with 22 separate units was popular during the war years and after. At Mrs. Fogelman's you could also rent a cot on the porch for one dollar per night.

The boarders shared a wood stove and an icebox, which often led to some heated arguments about who owned what. Particularly stressful were rainy days when all the women and their multitude of children were kept indoors and Friday nights when the women — all at once and in one small kitchen — decided to prepare a Sabbath supper for their husbands arriving on the eight o'clock train. For those who preferred a home-cooked meal at a restaurant, Fannie Mainster offered a kosher supper for $1.25 at her cottage — two hamburgers, two knishes and a bowl of borsht.

The Jewish presence at Winnipeg Beach was more formalized with the establishment of a synagogue in August 1950. The small log cabin blue and white synagogue at the corner of Hazel and Grove had enough room for about 75 worshippers. When it first opened, services were held Friday evening and Saturday morning but less and less people attended during the ensuing decades. Two years ago, when the Beach town council insisted that the synagogue install an expensive water and sewer hook-up, the synagogue's board decided instead to relocate the building to an empty lot down Gimli Road to Camp Massad. This proved to be a wise decision and the synagogue is again attracting Jewish residents for its Sabbath services.

Camp Massad has developed and promoted a consciousness and commitment among its campers and staff to Israel and Zionist ideals. At the same time, it was a camp, recalled Mrs. Billinkoff in 1993 on the occasion of the Massad's 40th anniversary, "where every little boy could learn to dance and every little girl to hammer a nail; where everyone could sing and appear on stage. It was important to teach Hebrew, but you also had to teach *menschlichkeit* — respect and goodness."

Winnipeg Jews still flock to the Beach each summer, though as their children move away from Winnipeg, there are a lot more cottages that sit empty during July and August. Winnipeg Beach — for better or for worse — is somewhat quieter now as families have replaced the hoards of teenagers who once ruled the town's main strip. ■

Winnipeg Beach had a host of attractions, including its famous roller-coaster and Boardwalk, to draw Winnipeggers of every class and ethnic background.

A young Christopher Dafoe (right) poses with friend outside his family's Ponemah cottage.

THE TWO MOST FAMOUS TRAINS on our side of the lake in those summers long ago were the "Moonlight" and the "Daddy's Train." The latter made two trips a day during the summer, picking up the working fathers just after dawn at the various stations down the line and getting them to jobs in Winnipeg well before nine. Wives in dressing gowns could be seen kissing their newly shaved husbands goodbye as the train pulled in. They made the return journey at 5:20 p.m. and the daddies, hot and frazzled after a busy day in town, got back to their cottages in time for a drink and a swim before dinner.

> There was always a crowd at the station at train-time and the scene was repeated at stations up and down the line: cars and wives waiting to pick up the arriving daddies...

Back in the 1940s the 5:20 train from Winnipeg also brought the daily papers — the *Tribune* and *Free Press* — and my brothers John and Peter and I, *Free Press* carriers at Ponemah, used to listen for the whistle and hoot that told us that the train, a roaring giant running on steam, was leaving Whytewold station. On our bikes, our bare feet pumping the pedals furiously, we raced the puffing train to the Ponemah station and usually lost by at least five car lengths.

There was always a crowd at the station at train-time and the scene was repeated at stations up and down the line: cars and wives waiting to pick up the arriving daddies; the local postmasters, who were also store-keepers, collecting sacks of mail and cartons of all-day suckers and pink popcorn from Winnipeg; children waiting for the train to pull out so that they could see what had happened to the pennies and bottlecaps they had left on the track to be flattened. There was a rumour, put about by grownups, that you could go to jail for putting coins on the track and flattening the king's face. It was also alleged that a coin on the track could derail the train, killing everyone aboard, but it never happened, although we put coins on the tracks all the time.

The Moonlight brought the dancers and fun-seekers down from Winnipeg early on Saturday evening and there were a few warm hours for dancing, walking along the Boardwalk; for riding the roller-coaster, the merry-go-round or the dodgem cars and eating hot dogs and "chips" at Eddie's Snack Bar and the Blue Bird Café.

The Moonlight, minus stragglers who often ended up sleeping on the beach, under the boardwalk or in the cells at the police station, left for the city on the stroke of midnight and it rolled through the beaches with a clatter, its riders already asleep or comfortably entwined. We used to run to the end of our street to watch the other trains pass, but we heard the Moonlight in our

sleep, a rapidly fading shriek in the thick and humming summer darkness as Sunday morning began.

By the early 1960s only a few freights used the old beach lines. The motor car was king. The summer stations were dismantled and the tracks rusted, but the Moonlight whistled on in memory, a ghost under the summer stars. Sometimes, even now, I hear it in the moment before sleep on a summer night, a thousand miles and more than half a century away.

The old Winnipeg Beach Boardwalk is gone as well. The merry-go-round, the dodgem cars, the naughty nickelodeons, the House of Horrors, the penny arcades and the arching roller-coaster that enchanted and terrified generations of Beach visitors were hauled away years ago. The Shetland ponies have vanished. The dance hall was dismantled, timber by timber. Only the beach remains — the long sandy curve sighted by Sir William in 1901 — and on hot summer weekends it is packed with people from the city and the surrounding countryside. Times and tastes

No matter what the weather, hundreds of Winnipeggers were drawn every weekend to the pavilion at Grand Beach.

PAM, Grand Baech 8

Tripping the Light Fantastic
at Lake Winnipeg Pavilions

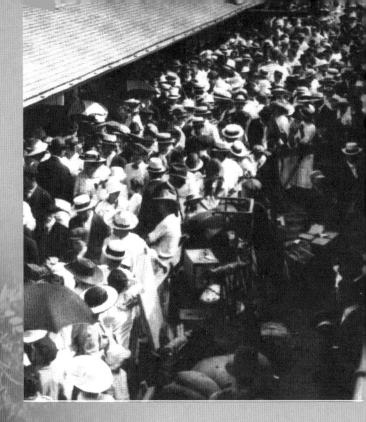

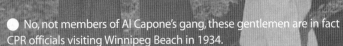

● No, not members of Al Capone's gang, these gentlemen are in fact
CPR officials visiting Winnipeg Beach in 1934.

PAM, Foote 1001

● Left: Throngs of Winnipeggers descended at Grand Beach to celebrate the weekend and dance at the Pavilion.

● Right: Musicians prepare for a weekend dance in the bandshell at the Grand Beach Pavilion.

● Below: Informal attire was discouraged at the Grand Beach Pavilion, as this 1918 photo clearly demonstrates.

National Archives of Canada, C33923

35

change, the pleasures of 1920 do not appeal in 2000. On the great lakes of Manitoba only the lake and the sand are exactly as they were.

The late nineteenth century lingered for an extra generation or two on Lake Winnipeg beaches. For a measure of years we rode our bikes over rumbling wooden sidewalks and played baseball on a field in Whytewold that was knee-deep in flowering weeds, sharing second base with a grazing cow. Coal oil lamps were common until well into the 1930s and were recalled to service for years after during electrical storms when the cottage lights flickered and went out.

On summer mornings you could smell poplar smoke as cottagers along the shore cooked eggs and bacon and burned toast on their wood-burning stoves. Ice was cut on the lake during the winter to keep soft drinks and Shea's Select cool in cottage iceboxes during the heat waves of July and August. The boys had the chore of carrying the ice water out of the cottage and it always spilled over the edge of the basin, soaking and freezing your feet.

Nick Dola was our ice and wood man and on summer afternoons in the early 1940s it was a treat to be allowed to sit beside him on his wagon as it moved in a cloud of dust along the Gimli Road hauling a load of cordwood to our cottage. The pungent aroma of the sweating horse, the formidable "Prince," combined with the dry, sharp smell of seasoned poplar was like the perfume of Arabia to a six-year-old nose, and when the wagon rolled into our yard, digging up the grass, it was an honour to be asked by Mr. Dola to help pitch the wood into the shed. Prince, standing patiently and flicking horseflies with his long, red tail, could be fed lumps of sugar, which he carefully took with his lips.

Other wagons and carts came to call as well: Ukrainian vegetable ladies with fresh corn-on-the-cob, beans, beets and garlic; Icelandic fishermen with pickerel fillets and Lake Winnipeg Goldeye at 25 cents a pound.

Down the road the formidable and widely beloved Madame Foures presided in *pince-nez* over the Ponemah store. She was not, we were told, "French Canadian," but transplanted from France itself, a warm-hearted character out of a novel by Colette or Flaubert, a fountain of local information and entertaining anecdote and

PAM, Winnipeg Beach 47

The pier at Winnipeg Beach, circa 1946.

Growing Up on Lake Winnipeg

BY SENATOR JANIS JOHNSON

Senator Janis Johnson with son Stefan and Snørri.

Like many Icelanders, I grew up on Lake Winnipeg. It was an ever-present power in my life. In the spring the ice melted, and water flooded over the dock and rolled onto Main Street in Gimli. It was considered to be a dangerous time and we were not allowed to go "downtown" alone. In the summer the wind sometimes whipped the lake into a raging ocean. We could play in the waves and this was heaven for my brothers and sisters. We spent hours riding the waves like surfers in California.

In the fall the lake would go very wild before the ice arrived. The waves would crash over the pier and again we were told "don't go near the dock" — a rule of life growing up in Gimli. Of course we did go on the dock, and saw incredible waves smashing across the decking during the rougher days.

If it was a stormy day and the fishing fleet had not returned the town would grow fearful. Men were lost every year on the lake so it was a nervous time. As a child, I often took solitary walks on the beach, and worried that I would find a drowned man washed up on the sand. In November the lake turned ghostly white, and was covered with icy snow for the next six months. It was too cold and windy to play or skate on. During the winter I could hardly wait for the sun to get hotter and melt the ice so I could do what I loved most — fishing.

I remember being a heartsick 10-year-old, jealous of the older boys who went fishing on the frozen lake in their Bombardiers. I was determined to become a fisherperson myself, and begged for a fishing rod for my birthday in April. I was so anxious, waiting for the big day, that I bit my nails to the quick. My city-bred parents were not anglers, and the boys in the neighbourhood were not sympathetic to my aspirations. They told me that girls were not supposed to fish. They didn't pester me too much though, because they knew I was a good fighter. There was a beautiful fishing rod for sale at Kardy's Hardware store and I've never wanted anything so badly in my life. "I really have to have my own rod," I explained to my parents with a plaintive wail. "That pathetic thing of dad's is useless!"

Persistence pays off. My parents gave me that fishing rod for my birthday, and I was ecstatic. It was bright red, and had a fine reel to go with it. I didn't have a minnow net, however, and on Lake Winnipeg, you need minnows to catch fish. The best place to get minnows was from the local boys, who would catch them with nets along the beach. Catching the tiny wriggling, silvery minnows was almost as much fun as going fishing. And it was a good excuse to get to know the boys.

So on the first warm day in spring, when the ice had finally melted, I came home from school and told my mother I was going fishing. I marched down Centre Street with my empty minnow can, my brand-new fishing rod, and my racing heart. I scrounged a few minnows from the local boys, and found myself a promising fishing spot halfway out on the dock. I picked out an unlucky minnow, carefully placed the hook through its mouth, gills and gut, then cast my line into the water. It was a glorious sunny afternoon and the harbour was quiet. A few fishing boats were moored at the old dock across the bay, and the "SS Goldfield" was leaving for the north. I owned the world and I knew it. A few hours later, my brother came to fetch me for dinner. I pulled the stringer from the water and showed him my fabulous haul. "Only three perch?" he asked. "What have you been doing all this time?"

I knew that he was only jealous, so I let him carry my fish as we walked home. "Now you just have to clean them," he said.

A few years later, a visitor came to our house and changed our lives forever. It was Premier Duff Roblin, and he wanted a favour from my dad. He wanted our dad (who eventually became Lieutenant Governor George Johnson) to run for the Tories in the next election. My dad was a well-loved country doctor who drove the muddy roads of the Interlake, delivering babies for a dollar apiece. He was elected, of course, because he'd taken the temperature of half the voters in the constituency, so we had to move to the city. And I was heartbroken. How would I live without my lake? Where would I walk? Where would I daydream? How could I ever replace the wild storms, the crackling ice, and the northern lights? Lake Winnipeg had turned me into a child of nature, and I didn't want to become a city girl.

But I had no choice. So I learned to live and work in an urban environment. But when I grew up, I inherited my grandmother's cottage in Gimli and I could be close to Lake Winnipeg. Underneath the power suit and high heels of my urban working costume there still lurks a girl with rubber boots and a fishing rod. And wherever I go, I carry the memory of that beautiful lake in my heart. ▪

Descendants of Icelandic immigrants still maintain fishing fleets on Lake Winnipeg.

Dave Reede

Building the last sandcastle of the day.

Dave Reede

repartee. She spoke an English that was roughly translated from the French, as on the occasion when she held us spellbound with a description of her husband Leo's heroic efforts to help save a nearby cottage that was burning down: "There was Leo," she exclaimed, "sawing away with an axe!"

Language was often a problem in those days, but never for long. Across the road from the Ponemah store was a large man of Slavic background who offered garden supplies for sale under the rubric "For Sell, Garden Sogel, Horse Manur." One afternoon while my mother was shopping and getting the news at the Ponemah Store my father decided to get a few bushels of "garden sogel" for the lawn. When my mother emerged from the store my father was still attempting to explain that he wanted 10 bushel baskets of garden soil, not a wagon-load of horse manure.

My mother joined them and attempted to bridge the language barrier with volume and hand gestures, the garden man displaying a degree of confusion as he looked from one to the other. Who was this woman and why was she butting in? Suddenly the light of understanding broke over his face: "Ah!" he said, "she's your misses!"

Tom Thomson

Observers can find a vast variety of birds on Manitoba's big lakes, including the bald eagle, the White pelican, and even the Double-crested cormorant.

Birding
the Lakes

BY GENE WALZ

The tiny Piping Plover, a pale, tawny-gray, black and white shorebird with flamboyant orange legs and feet, is so endangered that its nesting areas on the beaches of both great Manitoba lakes are fenced and protected.

The magnificent White Pelican and the gangly Double-crested Cormorant, both of which look like odd left-overs from the Jurassic Period, are so numerous on the province's lakes that they are sometimes slaughtered in misguided attempts to save fish.

The Three-toed Woodpecker, Sprague's Pipit, Connecticut Warbler, Great Grey Owl, LeConte's Sparrow, and Spruce Grouse, "must-see" birds on many international birders' wish-lists, are regular inhabitants of the boreal forests and grasslands around Clear Lake.

These are just some of the birds that make Manitoba one of the best birding spots in all of Canada. The province holds the record for the largest numbers of bird species seen during every month of the year from May through September.

Cottage country on the two big lakes (from Lynch's Point in the west to Delta Marsh at lake's end and around to St. Ambroise and Twin Lakes Beach on the east of Lake Manitoba and from Hecla Island down to Winnipeg Beach and around to Grand Marais and Traverse Bay on Lake Winnipeg) provides ample evidence of the wide range of species seen by lakeside birders. Ruby-throated Hummingbirds in the gardens, Baltimore Orioles in the tree-tops, eagles and ospreys and gulls overhead, dozens of ducks and geese and grebes on the water: birds are never far from sight, even from the porch or deck. Every vacationer in the province should have a pair of binoculars and a Peterson or National Geographic Fieldguide handy.

Of course, the best birds to look for at the lake are the non-city birds: the migrating shorebirds with the strange-sounding names (Avocets, Godwits, Phalaropes) in May and August, the loons on the lakes yodeling at dusk, herons and coots in the marshes, silent Gray Jays and chirpy Boreal Chickadees in the nearby forests, owls issuing the nightly warnings.

Delta Marsh and Oak Hammock are birding sites well worth special day trips. Every lake-site in Manitoba has its birding rewards. ■

After a sudden storm, a rainbow graces the horizon north of the pier at Hecla.

Dave Reede

Before 2,4-D and other dubious marvels of modern chemistry came along to strip the roadsides, you could pick wild raspberries along the ditches — making certain, always, to avoid the nettles. The woods along the roads were thick in August with saskatoon, pincherry, chokecherry and high bush cranberry. Family berry-picking parties, often numbering 20 or more pickers of all ages, used to range those mosquito infested woods armed with pails, pots, pans and sand buckets harvesting was what always a bumper crop, even with the birds in competition. You spent a lot of time looking up, and it was not uncommon to glance down and discover that you had blundered into a cow pie or a large bed of poison ivy. Once, an aunt sat down to rest on a large anthill, rising suddenly with a chorus of words that most of the younger children had never heard before. On one occasion, in a field far from home, we were chased by a farmer and two large, angry dogs, and made it to the car just in time, leaving behind us a trail of spilled chokecherries and a large sun hat belonging to an aunt. No one felt inclined to go back for the hat.

After the picking, however hot the day, the stoves were lit and mother and aunts sweated in hot kitchens preserving the harvest as jams and jellies. Through all the winter months we had a touch of summer sunshine on our toast every morning; cranberry jelly from Ponemah was served with the Christmas turkey in snowbound Winnipeg.

And then there were the storms! A sharp gust of wind always preceded a summer electrical storm. The air would become still, hardly a leaf would move and the silence was so complete that you could hear a mole running for shelter under the Hawthorne hedge in front of the cottage. Then the wind came, a short, sharp blast followed by the first distant rumble of thunder. Suddenly the rain was falling in torrents, sweeping off the lake, throwing up the sand and scattering leaves and dislodging dead branches. Darkness enveloped the summer community as we rushed to adjust awnings, close shutters and place buckets under leaks in the high roof.

The first crack of lightning almost made your hair stand on end. It was the end of the world; the whole sky was about to crash down and the

The Dafoe family cottage at Ponemah, circa 1950.

cottage shook. Water was seeping through the kitchen ceiling in two steady drips and wash basins and towels were arranged to catch the flow just as the lights flickered and the Irish tenor John McCormack on the gramophone became a basso profundo and fell silent.

The air above us shook and crashed. Somewhere out in the flooded yard a tree hurtled down with a loud rending of wood and a thump that shook the universe. The big water tank, full to the brim and beyond, churned like a wizard's cauldron.

The smaller children took refuge under the beds, dogs howled and cats cowered in corners. Veterans of summer storms settled down in chairs on the verandah to watch the show. The black sky over the lake was like a twenty-fourth of May fireworks display. Great bolts of thin and jagged fire flew from one end of the horizon to the other, illuminating the heaving water, glancing off the heaped clouds. The willows on the shore were bent flat.

You felt secure under the old timbers. The cottage had endured many storms and the chances were good that it would survive this one. Once a

Moody Manitoba **Monster**

BY DOUGLAS ALLEN

Lake country is the land of legends, myths, and — in the case of Lake Manitoba — monsters. Tales of a serpent-like creature in Lake Manitoba circulated for the better part of the last century. So many people reported seeing this creature that an amphibious scientific expedition was launched amidst wide-spread media coverage. The beast became so popular that it was given a name, and in the ultimate accolade for any self-respecting monster, a provincial park.

Manipogo, the name taken from Lake Okanagan's Ogopogo monster, was first sighted in 1909. Valentine McKay, an itinerant trapper canoeing on Cedar Lake, heard what sounded like thunder, and then saw a huge creature swimming ahead of him. Mr. McKay said that about four feet of its body was out of the water. The being disappeared behind an island.

Sightings were reported again in the '30s and '40s, and by the 1950s reports had become so numerous that an attempt to capture Manipogo was launched in September, 1957. Led by Solemn Fleury, the 19 member expedition set out from Lake Dauphin. Fleury had seen the monster on several occasions, and speculated that it used some caves at Steep Rock as a lair. Part of the team stumbled through two miles of muskeg to the cave Fleury had described. Inside the party found small animal bones, and a set of "weaving tracks" on the floor, but no other evidence.

Although nothing came of this expedition, sightings continued every year until the early 1960s when scientists from the University of Manitoba made two attempts to verify the existence of Manipogo. Dr. James McLeod's attempts were fruitless, but he did not rule out the possibility of some unknown creature inhabiting the lake.

Manipogo's zenith came in August of 1962, when Dick Vincent, a KCND newsman, not only saw the beast, but snapped a photo of it. Widely publicized, the picture showed a snake-like creature with a hump in the middle. The authenticity of the picture was never established, and in later years Vincent declined to comment further on the incident.

One of the difficulties in crediting these stories is the wide divergence in the various accounts. Manipogo is described as being both 15, and 40 feet long. Some said it had one hump, some said several. One report had it swimming at over 30 miles per hour, another claimed it moved slowly.

Although reported sightings of Manipogo have waned in recent years, it would pay to keep your eyes open on Lake Manitoba. You never know. ■

● Is Manipogo still lurking somewhere in these calm Lake Manitoba waters?

Dave Reede

tree fell on our mercifully unoccupied outdoor biffy, but the old cottage was charmed. We sat happily, wrapped in blankets while the rain hammered down on the shingle roof and gushed along the ditches into the lake. Then the storm passed as suddenly as it had come and the wide August sky was ablaze with shooting stars.

Our first boats on the lake were rafts, lengths of pier timber with green, waxy bark and logs nailed together with pieces of driftwood and old weather-beaten two-by-fours found among the sea-wrack on the shore. They floated precariously just below the surface of the water and the novice sailor had to wear a bathing suit, or soak his jeans. The mast, nailed insecurely and liable to collapse at any moment, supported a pirate flag drawn with charcoal on a torn piece of pillow-case.

We drifted up and down the shallow shore water in search of Treasure Island, our swords fashioned out of willow saplings, the enemy waiting in ambush around the next patch of reeds. Waterlogged and sluggish, the *Hispaniola*, out of Ponemah Beach via Havana, patrolled the shoreline, making war with passing gulls and motorboats.

Later the pirate crew graduated into a red canoe and, although cautioned not to, sought the deeper waters far from shore, then tipped over, accidentally on purpose.

When the waves rolled too high for seafaring, there was a snug fort hidden deep in the willows with a campfire ringed with stones and a cool larder hollowed out of the moist sand and well stocked with chocolate, marshmallows and grog (the latter sold commercially at the Ponemah Store under the trade names Wynola, Kik, Stubby Lemon-lime and Wishing Well Orange).

On dark nights when the fishflies swarmed and died under the lamp posts along the Gimli Road we sat in a circle of light by the fire toasting marshmallows and wieners on sharpened willow branches while the sparks danced high in the air like fireflies. When the ashes cooled there were baked potatoes under the cinders, their coats charred black, the moist flesh delicious with salt and butter.

The pirates of long-lost summers have joined the older generations on the croquet lawn or in deck chairs on the sand, but new bands of pirates can be seen by the shore, messing about on

Dave Reede

Hikers enjoy the untouched beauty of the limestone cliffs near Steep Rock, on Lake Manitoba.

In Their Own Words:
Victoria Beach

BY PAUL VINCENT (AS TOLD TO DOUGLAS ALLEN)

*P*aul Vincent is a life-long cottager at Victoria Beach. He is currently a lumberjack in the Charlevoix region of Quebec.

"My parents bought our Victoria Beach property in 1945, the year I was born. There was a cottage that was built by the original owner, which we used until the late '70s, when it was torn down. We all hated to see it go, but my parents wanted to use the property in the winter, and the old place had no foundation.

I spent every July and August at the cottage, and weekends during the school year. I basically lived on the beach in front of the cottage….Boats have never been a big part of Victoria Beach cottage life but Dad had boats from the day he bought the property. One of the highlights of the summer was the times we would go to the cottage by boat….Saturday morning, we would load up the boat, and set out on the Red by mid-morning. It was a leisurely cruise, unlike some of the trips I would make later!

Once we got to the lake, we would get about half way across to Victoria, and if the water was calm, Dad would shut off the motor, and we would float, and have lunch. The whole trip usually took about four hours, which was the same time it took to drive. It was during these trips that I learned to navigate through Netley Marsh, a skill that stood me in good stead.

Dad eventually acquired a Donzi, an Italian-made fiberglass ocean racing boat. It was only 17 feet, but it weighed 2,000 pounds, and could take as much punishment as Lake Winnipeg in a temper could dish out. That much boat around you instills a lot of confidence, and I occasionally tackled water that would give me pause today. One instance in particular sticks in my mind. It was the May long weekend, about ten years ago.

Two friends and I decided to make the trip, and we were in such a hurry that I didn't bother to get a marine forecast for the south basin. I had an inkling of what lay in store, because there was a fairly stiff breeze out of the northwest. We had a great trip until we got into the lake. Then we saw the whitecaps! As we got closer, it became obvious that this was going to be a wild ride. The waves were a good six feet, and the wind was howling, to say nothing of the fact that at that time of year, any mishap would almost certainly have been fatal. So, a vote was taken, and the decision was to go for it. Fortunately the waves were coming on the beam so I was able to get the Donzi up on the crests, and we skipped all the way to the cottage. I was glad my parents weren't there when we arrived!

I also made the trip once at night, which was even more hairy. Getting through the marsh in the dark was quite tense, as I couldn't see the channels, and the weight of the Donzi would have made it impossible to free it if I had run aground. It was worth it when we got to the lake. The moon was shining, and there was only a slight swell. That was a memorable crossing.

Some of the best memories of my life are associated with Victoria Beach, and going by boat has always been a highlight." ■

48

rafts and swinging high in the branches of old trees. A great-nephew is among them, scabs on both knees and out at the elbows, a sword clutched in his brown hand, a drooping moustache brushed on with charcoal from last night's bonfire.

I know exactly what he is going to do next. I have done it myself and my father did it before me. In a moment his mother is going to warn him that he could break his neck, just as my mother warned me, my wife warned our children and my grandmother warned my father.

Sitting in my chair, comfortable and 30 years out of condition, I feel an impulse to climb that old tree again, to go right to the top to see if my initials are still carved on the bark. But another child climbs instead and our hands reach out to touch the blue edge of the sky. There are children at the beach every summer, year after year; essentially the same children, playing the same games.

One summer rolls into another so easily that the events of many summers become jumbled together, forming a muddled pattern of memory: cool swims before breakfast with a bar of Ivory soap; family picnics at the Point; Saturday nights at Winnipeg Beach circumnavigating the Boardwalk;

Dave Reede

Cyclists admire the view overlooking Lake Winnipeg at Hecla.

49

bicycle rides along the dusty road to Matlock for the Saturday Dance with Harold Greene and his Orchestra; competitions to see who could walk all the way to Whytewold Station along the railroad track without falling off; poison ivy; sunburn; skunks encountered on the path to the biffy; the "honey-wagon" rattling down our street by moonlight; birthday parties; kissing girls; burning leaves in the autumn, once nearly burning my Uncle Ted's DeSoto when I lit a small fire to burn off grass by the side of the road; singing the old songs — *Silvery Moon, Moonlight Bay* and *There's a Long, Long Trail* — around the bonfire with the sparks flying high; the Northern Lights; the *Keenora* passing by far off shore; tennis marathons that continued until it was so dark that you could hardly see the ball; the 1939 August long-weekend sailing race that was struck by a sudden storm that turned the boats over one by one. Nobody drowned but some of the survivors drank all my father's whisky and borrowed the new trousers he was planning to wear on a holiday in Yellowstone Park. Years and years pile up around the old cottage like drifting leaves or memories. Time passes and the children who sailed rafts along the shore see their own children and grandchildren playing the same games under the

Helgoland Redux

BY INGEBORG BOYENS

The picture in the family photo album shows me as a toddler, marching in my handmade coat up the gangway of the *S.S. Homeric.* The invisible hands holding me are those of my mother, smiling uneasily in vampy red lipstick and of my father, wearing the trench coat and fedora of the times. Our going-to-Canada clothes. The hand that took that photo was steady, but it was documenting a farewell. This is the image of my little family's final day of life in Germany and the beginning of life as immigrants to the New World.

It was the late 1950s, the time of a great wave of immigration from Europe to Canada. With a child's self-absorption, I knew little of my parents' subsequent scramble for jobs, shelter, and food in our new home in Winnipeg. It was not until I went to school that I discovered German was something you only spoke at home. That began my own singular resolve to fit into the Canadian way.

As the years passed, my parents managed to afford the essentials of life and then began to look to the extras. We moved from the North End to the south part of town. We sampled our first steak. We purchased a car — a little VW Beetle of course — at a time when it was simply cheap transportation, not a fashion statement. With what I later recognized as the German quest for "nature", we packed up a canvas tent, Coleman stove and the other fundamentals of camping, and explored Manitoba's lake country.

Clearing the bush in preparation for the building of the first cottages at Helgoland.

With immigrant thoroughness, we pitched our tent and dipped a fishing line just about everywhere — at West Hawk, Twin Beaches, Manigotagan, and finally Camp Neustadt north of Gimli on Lake Winnipeg. There were usually other German immigrants around, a society of sorts within the broader Canadian life. For me, "the lake" was a place where I would not be taunted for being a "Kraut," where my thick blonde pigtails were not an oddity, where my mother's sewing skills did not illicit the ridicule of the fashion-conscious.

I was 14 when my parents took that first tentative step to cottage ownership. Along with some friends, they bought 32 acres on the beach not far from Camp Neustadt from the Helgasons, a family of Icelandic fishermen who viewed the lake pragmatically as a source of economic wealth. It cost $7,500. By today's standards it seems a pittance but for newcomers to Canada, used to making do with little, it was a small fortune.

The enterprise needed a name. They dubbed it "Helgoland" after the red rock island in the North Sea that has been a mythic place in German culture throughout its tumultuous history.

We had subtly stepped into the makings of a more monied class. But immigrant habits of scrabbling for money died hard. My parents pitched the tent under a large spruce tree, in a dry spot in what was otherwise waterlogged poplar bush. And they set about clearing the land by hand, with axe and saw. There are no pictures of this time, for documenting hard work would have been unseemly. My mother apparently went everywhere with axe in hand, ready to attack some recalcitrant bush or sapling. The Rotchiess (we all called them Opa and Oma for they were in their sixties) are captured in my memory stripped down to sweaty undershirts, each bent over an end of a Swedish saw.

It was two years before a road was built, and longer still before such luxuries as a well, hydro, and a telephone line appeared. Until then, the VW, piled high with lumber and supplies, trundled impossibly through the bush for half a mile to the lakefront. Our cottage kit was unceremoniously dumped at the end of the road at the closest neighbours. When one of our crew cut his foot with a poorly aimed axe, he was rattled along in a wheelbarrow to the Helgasons' house where the ambulance could collect him.

While my parents were clearing land with the same fervour shown by the country's original homesteaders, I was living a life of pure release. My summertime friends were a group of girls of about the same age. We shared a fundamental characteristic — we were a generation with one foot in the New World and another in the old. Those were summers of few rules, few recriminations, few ethnic embarrassments. While our parents worked, we were on the beach, working on our sunburns, labouring hard to swamp the canoe, toiling to stay heads-up while a windy day's surf crashed down on us at the shore edge.

Now, nearly 30 years later, there is nothing raw anymore about Helgoland. Fuelled by neighbourly competitiveness, it boasts fruitful gardens, neat lawns and tidy sprawling cottages that have grown with the years. The swampy patches have been drained by carefully placed ditches. The forest of black poplars has been replaced by a pleasing assortment of white birch, spruce, larch and Russian elm.

There are cottages up and down the big lake now, developed by contractors, bulldozers and chainsaws. The sprucewood forest to the south that triggered the imaginations of youngsters raised on the Brothers Grimm is now a cottage development with neat public spaces where children can ride their bikes.

These days, my German is a rusty memory. The back-wrenching toil of my parents' immigrant generation is past. And yet, when I go to my version of Helgoland, I swear that — amongst the sights and smells of Manitoba — I can taste North Sea salt on the wind off the lake. ■

old oaks and birches. The August moon, a huge orange ball in the eastern sky, notes the changes that the years bring, is aware of arrivals and departures, marks the turning of many happy summers and the slow passing of a century.

The summer communities along Lake Winnipeg, abandoned by the railway, flourished again with the motor car. The grey lake, which once saw only the passage of Indian canoes and York boats and the Icelandic fishing fleet, is bright on July afternoons with the sails of windsurfers. Attempts to create grand resorts on the great sandbars at the south end of Lake Winnipeg, including the ambitious "Sans Souci" project of the 1930s, were unable to contend with high water, but cottages perch there to this day, linking east and west sides of the lake along the Red River Delta and the Salammaniac Channel. People continue to argue about the best use of the old resorts, but while proposals for the creation of "world-class destinations," grand hotels, golf courses and other tourist inducements appear from time to time in Saturday editions of the local papers, ordinary

Manitobans continue to enjoy the simple pleasures provided by nature herself: the beaches, the lakes, and the two golden months of sunshine and warm winds. Some prefer Lake Manitoba, others choose the west or the east side of Lake Winnipeg. Family traditions are often involved and loyalty can be intense.

"The beach" is as comfortable as a favourite pair of shoes, as familiar as your grandmother's face.

The beaches are Winnipeg's back garden, its favourite destination, its second home. The great dance hall burned down long ago, but large crowds still enjoy Grand Beach, once dubbed one of North American's finest strips of golden sand by *Playboy* magazine. Victoria Beach is still a place where you can walk in the middle of the road without fear of cars or bask on a beach cooled by a breeze blowing lightly off the lake or bump into people you once knew at school. Hecla Island is

still peaceful and remote, although you can get there by car and it has become a popular Provincial Park, attracting tourists from across Canada. Gimli, still the place for fish and oldtime country stores, has also become a water sports centre with an international reputation. Cottages still line the shores, although more and more people are living at the lake all year in modern houses or making it a year-round resort, with ice-fishing, cross-country skiing and curling at the local rink. "The beach" is as comfortable as a favourite pair of shoes, as familiar as your grandmother's face. People have always liked it that way and hope it never becomes too posh or too civilized. Old Manitoba lives at the lake and the passing of a century is like the passing of a summer day or the swift flight of a shore bird in a blue sky. ∎

Dave Reede

LAKES OF THE
HIGHLANDS

The Riding Mountain/
Turtle Mountain Region

BY DAWN GOSS

Drawing his big toe through the sand, a tourist standing on the beach at Clear Lake says to me "It's really nice here, but where's the mountain?" Out on the water, a trio of loons laughs out loud. "You're on it," I say.

In all fairness to the gracious newcomer, he wasn't the first one to ask the question. The gradual drive up the slope from Brandon had disguised the elevation, and Riding Mountain isn't really a mountain anyway, but rather an escarpment, a lush green wedge jutting 350 metres above the flat farmland of southwestern Manitoba. The height of the plateau at the top of Riding Mountain can only be appreciated from the north and east where steep slopes rise dramatically from the surrounding prairie.

RIDING MOUNTAIN, WITH ITS PATCHWORK of forest, prairie and water-filled glacial depressions, as well as Duck Mountain to the north, are segments of a long string of highlands in western Manitoba known collectively as the Manitoba Escarpment. The highlands, and the broad valleys that separate them, have a similar shale core that was formed 60 to 130 million years ago. Rivers and advancing glaciers wore away areas of softer shale. As the last glacial ice melted some 12,000 years ago, ancient Lake Agassiz was formed — lapping along the escarpment. Four thousand years later, it drained northeast into Hudson Bay, leaving successive beach ridges paralleling the foot of the escarpment. This also applies to "the Ducks" — a hilly terrain of irregular deposits of clay, gravel, sand and boulders that includes a series of lakes like Wellman, Child, Singush and The Blues, not to mention big hills — Baldy Mountain being the highest at 831 metres.

To the south, close to the American border, a deeper layer of rock-black shales and limestone formed a foundation for the same shale layer deposited in Riding and Duck Mountain. A final layer — a mantle of glacial till — was responsible for Turtle Mountain. As buried chunks of ice thawed there was considerable shifting and collapse of the land above them, causing many hills and water-filled depressions — now known as Adam, Max, William, George and Bower Lakes. As the glacier receded, the water contracted into flowing streams — the Pembina, which cut a chain of lakes like Pelican, Lorne, Louise, Rock and Swan — and Long River, one of its most spirited tributaries, which chiseled out a deeper bed now known as Killarney Lake.

Since it was the first dry land that appeared after the glacial period, the Turtle Mountain region is the oldest known inhabited part of the province. According to some Aboriginal creation stories, the glacier pulled back, the turtle expanded and the world was created. Turtle Mountain is a natural border between a northern ecosystem and a southern one with two huge drainage areas, one going to the Arctic, and one going to the Gulf of Mexico. Because it was a natural border between those ecosystems, it was also a border between cultures and economies.

 A wide range of Aboriginal tribes, including the Assiniboine, the Cree and the Ojibway, lived and hunted in the highlands of western Manitoba.

PAM

To the north there was an Algonquin federation of Cree and Ojibway and Saulteaux with a few allies like the Assiniboine. To the south — a broad Siouan federation with Lakota, Dakota, most of the Yanktons and Mandans, and their allies the Cheyenne. It was an area shared by many, so Turtle Mountain became a natural place to conduct mediation and to trade and conduct common ceremony. There are several archeological sites to verify this.

Farther to the north, the Woodland Cree, in some of their favourite hunting grounds, lived in the highlands. The Assiniboine, on the surrounding prairie, trailed the path of the bison herds. Families settled around Riding Mountain's lakes on a seasonal basis to fish and hunt and, like present-day visitors, they picked the best campsites — like the open east end of Lake Audy, the beaches of Deep Lake and Moon Lake, and the shores around Clear Lake.

The Duck Mountain area was well known to Assiniboine, Cree and Anishinabe (Ojibway) who hunted elk and moose there, trapped beaver and other fur-bearing animals. The Pine River Trail which cuts across the northern part of "the Ducks"

was one of their travel routes. Campsites known as teepee sites are located around the mountain, one of the most prominent being at Singush Lake along the creek.

More than 500 generations of nomadic hunters have thrived in "the mountains" and surrounding areas. Explorers and fur traders took advantage of native guides, waterways, trails and

campsites to secure the western expansion of their trade. By the late 19th century the bison herds were gone, as were the grizzly and woodland caribou. Regional native bands were moved to reserves. Rail lines stretched inexorably west and north, bringing new immigrants, slowly at first, then in their multitudes. With the horse and the plough, these new Canadians laid their own

National Archives of Canada, C3569

New settlers, many from eastern Europe, quickly transformed the western Manitoba prairie into a rich agricultural region.

● Lake Clementi was the favourite summer playground for Brandon's developing middle class.

foundations and, in the process, redefined the southwestern Manitoba landscape.

There are many examples. Reminded of the celebrated lakes of his homeland, an Irish immigrant and government land agent, John Sydney O'Brien, retrieves from his tent a bottle of "the Irish" — and christens Killarney Lake. Settlers are soon drawn to the village at the east end of this four-mile lake. Not far away, while cutting wood on the Turtle's back, five Williams — William Ryan, William Shannon, William Boyd, William Hewitt and William Anderson stumble on a quiet lake that would later be enjoyed by many. Not surprisingly they name it William Lake and make good use of the abundant berries and fish. Closer to the Turtle's head, land surveyor Otto Klotz names Max Lake after his son. All manner of homelands or trees or emotions or family members or even pets qualify as namesakes for these aqua puzzle-pieces flashing in the prairie sun.

Lured by the Manitoba and North Western Railway, newcomers flooded areas like Strathclair and nearby Salt Lake. John Norquay, Premier of Manitoba, enjoyed a summer home on the northeast corner of Salt Lake which quickly became a popular picnic and resort spot. He planned to have a sanatorium/resort erected there because of the apparent health properties of the mineral salts in the lake, but died suddenly in 1888 before he was able to complete his plans.

Railway advertisements entitled "Summer Tours" with descriptions of resorts, drew middle-class Winnipeggers to holiday at Shoal Lake northwest of Minnedosa, Sabbath School rail-picnickers were lured to Canadian Pacific points like Plum Creek (Souris) and Oak Lake. Destinations like Killarney and Lake Clementi in the Brandon Hills become attractive to picnickers and even a few early cottage owners.

Local lakes and rivers become popular — like the Little Saskatchewan River — better known as "The Dam" to Brandonites and which would become the scene of numerous camping-out parties of guides and scouts. The Dam itself — the first hydro-electric plant in western Canada — would be one of many water reserves including Minnedosa and Rivers to appeal to heat-fatigued locals.

Logging in the Duck Mountains in the 1920s. (Painting by Marion Barker from photograph.)

By the turn of the century, the mountains became important sources of timber to incoming settlers. Portable mills in "the Ducks" and fixed mills at Grandview and Swan River made logging the area's major industry, supplying would-be farmers with the needed cash to buy equipment, stock and seed. In Riding Mountain, logging became so extensive that the Dominion Government created a Timber Reserve, issuing permits in an attempt to curb overcutting. The next decade, it was changed to a Forest Reserve and a forest ranger was hired, but poaching and excessive timber cutting continued. In an effort to address issues surrounding logging, the inspector of the Forest Reserve advocated that by creating a summer resort at Clear Lake, those having summer residences would take an active role in the protection and preservation of the land and forest.

In 1908 Ludwig Gusdal packed up his horses and moved from Erickson to Clarke's Beach (later Wasagaming). The trip took him three days. Eight years later he filed the first surveyed lot, then built the first cottage "Kumbekumfy". By 1918 several more beach lots would be taken, and facilities and access roads built.

THE SAME IMPULSE TO RECREATION was being felt farther south. As the largest navigable body of water in southwestern Manitoba, Pelican Lake drew a sizable population of summer tourists — campers and railway daytrippers. Part of the appeal was boating — including a 60-foot double-decker steamer and a flotilla of various crafts of all shapes and sizes.

The western lakes soon were filled with various floating vessels transporting people to resorts and cottage destinations — the *Anemone* on Shoal Lake, the *Lady of the Lake* on Max Lake, the *Shamrock* on Killarney Lake. With the influx of people, new problems arose. The town council in

Killarney passed a motion: "That our policeman, Walter Brown, be notified to apprehend any person or persons who are found on or around the shores of Killarney Lake...exposing themselves indecently, or without bathing suits, or undressing in the open where they may be seen, and to have all such persons brought before the authorities and prosecuted for such offense."

During the 1920s, beach resort facilities at Killarney, Rock Lake and Max Lake in the Turtle Mountains drew all classes of daytrippers and cottagers. Flapper fashion-plates donned an array of "questionable" swimming attire. Automobiles

became more popular and plans were afoot to spend two million dollars on good roads throughout 16 municipalities. Enthusiasm was increasing for a national park development to the north with "much greater the accommodation and recreational possibilities than could be found at Lake Clementi, Oak Lake or Ninette." In 1929, the

The clean, cool air surrounding Pelican Lake provided an ideal environment for the Ninette Sanatorium.

federal government authorized Riding Mountain to be developed as Manitoba's first national park. Unfortunately, this move had to be delayed as plummeting stock values on the North American exchanges, signaling the Depression, combined with high unemployment put a damper on development.

Going to the lake during that era "means different things to different people in different ages" according to long-time George Lake cottager Peter Stobbe. As a boy living outside Turtle Mountain, the 1930s were much less recreational oriented than survival oriented:

"By the mid '30s I was already a man of nine years old. And I recall going back to mow hay with my brother and my father and there were millions of flies and mosquitoes and they were after your hide...we camped on our hay rack...My father had a rental property on the lake shore and because the water had receded — the grass was encroaching on the old lake bottom...it was totally dry...and I remember mowing that...and all of a sudden the ski (on the mower) jerked, I stopped the horses and looked back and here I had hooked onto a buffalo skull and it was huge...I don't recall

Two women model the latest in fashionable beach attire at Oak Lake near Virden, circa 1900.

PAM, N17637

finishing the mowing but I recall coming home from the 'hay lake' with this great treasure. Coming back from the hay meadows we always went past 'Fish Lake' (sometimes called Holmes Lake) — of course the horses...had to stop there...and while we were there, there was just enough time for a...skinny dip...and I don't know if you can imagine how pieces of hay stick in the heat and your body is just covered with itch and into a cool lake was — just wonderful."

Unemployment was on the rise — a government survey reported 7,000 Manitobans without work. The provincial government picked up on the idea of work camps and by 1932 national work camps were also established. By 1934 more than 25,000 men had joined the 'Royal Twenty Centres' in remote camps in the wilderness across the country. At this time, a camp in newly named Wasagaming, the Cree name for "clear water", housed hundreds of workers — making roads, doing beach work, and building government facilities including a museum, a theatre and a 700-foot breakwater.

PAM, N13953

The vast variety of wildlife found in Riding Mountain National Park attracted visitors from across the country.

When the Lake is a River

BY CAROL PRESTON

● The Lamont family on a Sunday outing to the Souris River, circa 1939.

In the 1920s, when Ada and Archie Lamont and their five children settled on a farm near the town of Margaret in southwestern Manitoba, vacations were not part of their life. The Lord's Day was a day of rest, however, and so early on fine Sunday afternoons in the summertime, the family would hitch their horses Connie and Bing to the wagon and head north across the prairie towards the valley of the Souris River.

One popular recreation spot along the river was Riverside Park at Highway 10, where businessmen from Brandon had built a dance pavilion, and a ballpark that featured some excellent baseball teams. Usually though, the family favoured a more isolated location about five kilometres northeast of their farm. As they descended the steep ravine leading to the valley floor, they would often see deer, and occasionally they met Aboriginals from North Dakota who camped by the Souris on their way to perform at the Brandon Fair.

During the many hot dry years of the twenties and thirties, the best picnic spot was at a bend in the river, by a shallow crossing used at one time by the farmers of southwestern Manitoba to haul their grain by wagon to Brandon, 45 kilometres to the north. Here the family spread blankets in the shade of the elms and Manitoba maples, and enjoyed a few rare hours of leisure.

Sometimes they were joined by neighbours, and frequently during the 1920s by nurses from the "San" at Ninette where low water levels had made Pelican Lake unpleasant for swimming. For mixed bathing everyone changed into suits in the bushes, and swam in cool water under a shale bank in the deepest part of what they called "the bay." The most common swimming stroke was the "dog paddle," and the bathing costumes were far from stylish (son Donald recalls that his wool swimsuit, ventilated by a few moth-holes, had tight legs and a skirt, which floated up in the water).

Other popular activities included birdwatching, fishing for northern pike using willow branches for rods, and picking berries such as saskatoons, pin cherries and highbush cranberries that were an important addition to the family's food supply.

Late in the afternoon, a fire was made of dried branches, and when the coals were red, they fried home-made sausages in a cast-iron frying pan. These were eaten with home-made rolls, followed by cake or pie, and washed down with lemonade. After dinner the family relaxed around the fire, their conversation punctuated by the occasional splash as the fish started jumping in the early evening, a sign that it was time to pack up and head for home where there were animals waiting to be fed, and cows to be milked. ■

ON SEPTEMBER 10, 1939, CANADA declared war on Germany. The war had its effects even in the cottage country of western Manitoba. From 1943 to the end of World War II, more than 400 German prisoners of war were detained at a camp on the east side of Whitewater Lake in Riding Mountain National Park. The guards didn't bother themselves with rifles and fences, given that the few escape attempts that were made ended with the escapees getting lost and timidly finding their way back again. Life wasn't too distasteful at the POW camp — the prisoners had their own orchestra, choir, gardens, and kept pigs and pets, including one bear cub.

Long-time residents of the area remember the war period well. Boris Hryhorczuk has a home on Child's Lake; he spent his early years in "The Ducks" in a log cabin with his parents and his grandparents:

"During the war there were all kinds of airports through the prairies as part of the Commonwealth Air Training Program...students came from all over the Commonwealth — New Zealand, Australia...Dad was a fairly prominent citizen in Ethelbert and he spearheaded the war bond sales...and he became quite friendly with some of the base commanders and pilots — they used to fly these Harvards — the training horse of the Commonwealth and they made an awful lot of noise. Dad...used to invite a few pilots over to our place at the cabin for the weekend. They'd fly over Ethelbert and drop a little parachute with a note in it saying 'Coming up to the lake this weekend if it's okay.' So one time one of these little notes said 'Mike if you're on East Blue this weekend, we're going to get you!' We had this big Peterborough canoe...so we took up the challenge and we went out and Dad says 'Boris — you keep you eyes on the skyline.' Sure enough...up over the trees at the end of the lake came three Harvards and...I can remember the tops of the spruce trees waving and they dipped down onto the lake, their propellers splashing water as they went and they headed right for the boat. Dad turned toward shore and VROOOOOOOOOM!"

English war bride at Clear Lake, 1947.

Sailing with Dad on Pelican Lake

BY MARTHA BROOKS

"The sailboat had been hauled up in October and stored in the boathouse, but with continued mild weather I had put off taking in the wharf to save it from the spring break-up. Now in late November snow blanketed the frozen lake. Mild weather, however, continued and on a late Sunday afternoon, with no sanatorium visitors around to be interviewed, my thoughts turned, as always, to the lake and, in particular, to the neglected wharf.

A sniff of my old clothes told the dogs they were in for a tramp, and shortly we were on the scene and I was busy with crowbar and nail puller. The heavy spikes squealed in the still air as they pulled out of wood, but the planking came off without great difficulty and was soon stored in the boathouse. The oak posts, now solidly frozen in the ice, would have to be left. A brief inspection inside the boathouse in the dimming light showed a damaged rudder and a broken boom that would need repairing during winter nights before the little craft would again slip down the runway to another season of footing her way through the restless waters of Pelican Lake."

A woodcut rendered by Dr. A.L. Paine.

"The Lake," a short memoir published in the February 1948 issue of *The Messenger of Health*, calls up the voice of its author, my beloved father A. L. Paine, rural surgeon and — to my unjaundiced eye — Renaissance man. The family lived on the grounds of the Manitoba Sanatorium, in hills overlooking Pelican Lake, and for many years Dad was the only sailor on its waters. Our house, with its wraparound verandah and expansive screened-in sleeping porches, captured a delicious breeze even on the hottest of July nights. That kind of welcome coolness is a familiar memory to anyone who is lucky enough to escape to a lakeside summer cottage. However, we lived by the water year round, so our experience involved a seasonal cycle that bore witness to everything from sun haze to sun dogs.

Here is a memory of my father and me, at seven, tramping through the deep snow with our tag-along four-footed pals. It's Sunday afternoon, a couple of hours before suppertime. We walk past the boathouse, snowshoes strapped to our moccasins, and take to the lake. Dad's probably whistling. The dogs' coats are ice crusted. A scarf is wrapped around my face. Only a couple of minutes out one of my snowshoes comes away. Suddenly entangled in the thick lampwick strapping, I fall over and let out a yelp. Dad turns back. During his efforts to extricate me, the dogs lurch in to lick my eyelids. He tries elbowing them

Dr. Paine, Martha Brooks' father, enjoys a quiet moment on his sailboat.

out on the verandah, varnishes the boat and occasionally glances over his shoulder at the cold lake beyond the newly leafed trees. Counting the days, likely, until he's out on the water, with or without us. Mom brings him coffee, leans girlishly against the verandah railing. My sister, inside the house, waits for her longtime boyfriend. Our grandparents move slowly around in their upstairs room. I take off, by myself, into the hills that skirt the rim of the valley. The solitary pleasure of sinking into nature has not, even at the age of ten, escaped me. The hills, as they say, are alive.

Summer. The usual water-up-your-nose plunges off the dock. Also lazy paddles, with Dad, past cutbanks filled with nesting swallows that dive and swoop around the overhanging lush growth: saskatoon and chokecherry bushes, leaf-clattering aspens. Picnic-bound, the family often sails down the lake, a basket filled with devilled eggs, sliced ham, pickles, buns, and that peculiarly Canadian delicacy, raisin-filled butter tarts.

September. Monday. Mom and Dad have walked down the road to tend to their tuberculosis patients. My sister has gone back to University. The grandparents speak softly to each other, in Icelandic, as I run out the door for school at the village of Ninette. During the days to come, there will be chilly tramps along the beach and corn roasts on the hillsides, as leaves turn gold in the rising smoke of autumn. At our house we will sometimes dream of summer, but always in the reassuring presence of Pelican Lake.

"I paddle to the centre of the lake and there sleep at anchor with a blanket and the sails for covering and the dogs at my feet. Hours later we are awakened by the lap of small waves against the boat and arise to find the moon is up, bringing with it a steady night breeze, fragrant with the scent of sweet clover. Morning is not far off and may bring another hot still day, so now before it comes is the time to sail. These night breezes arriving with a late rising moon are the most perfect of all for sailing. They are so steady and free from squalls that one can set the sail, lash down the rudder and wander at ease about the deck. Now we slip along through the warm night at a steady pace that eats up the miles. The bow cuts cleanly through the smooth waves, and with water gurgling quietly under her belly the little craft steers for home, leaving a long moonlit track of gleaming bubbles in her wake." ▬

away as we laugh, helplessly. The dogs finally leap back and bark in unison. They want to go. They are eager to explore the islands of frozen bullrushes and shoreline of bare-limbed oaks and snow-humped rocks, all under this late-day January sky with apricot light descending.

Spring. Some other Sunday. Crabapple blossoms shake in the wind against the kitchen window, and the sky is a bright May-time blue. Dad,

A young Martha poses with her mom and dad on the grounds of the Ninette Sanatorium.

PAM, Killarney Lake 4

But there's an extension to the story:

"...families had come up after Sunday church — this bunch of farmers (suspenders), white shirts...Sunday pants type of thing and a few of the adult fellows had climbed this diving tower... about 15 feet high...and these guys are standing on the diving board watching the lake when these Harvards came in — right at them and buzzed them, and they all jump off this thing right into the water in their Sunday best!...I'm sure if they were found out they (the pilots) would somehow have their wings stripped from their lapels...but these were the war years — '40 to '45, fairly short lived period in our history but they had their impact up here in the Duck Mountains."

Killarney Lake, circa 1956.

In Their Own Words:
East Blue Lake

BY VIOLET PLOSHYNSKY (AS TOLD TO DAWN GOSS)

Violet Ploshynsky cottages in an old log Relief Camp dining hall on Singush Lake in 'The Ducks.' She and her husband Bill owned and operated a confectionery at East Blue Lake. This story occurred in 1961.

"A forestry fellow found an orphaned deer about so high (foot and a half) and...came to the store and asked if we were interested in looking after it and well of course we were. But the first thing that Bill (her husband) did was build a wire pen and found out immediately that you can't pen up a little wild animal. So he was on the loose. We fed it with a bottle and a nipple, named him "Bambi" of course. And he used to chase the children on the beach and play with them like a dog would. But Bambi found a place to sleep in a grove of trees across the highway from the store — not anywhere where there were people. But in the morning, Bambi would be at our doorstep, if he wasn't we would call his name and he would come. That was the year of the forest fire, it was '61-62. So anyway we had to evacuate because it was so close to the store — about 1/4 mile from East Blue Lake. But I went out on the highway to call Bambi but I couldn't for the lump in my throat, I couldn't call him at all.

Anyway, the next day my husband went back up with the truck and Bambi was small enough, he called Bambi, he got him and he tied his feet together — he had to — but he brought him home (to Ethelbert) on the front seat of the truck. And we let him loose. We had a big yard with a clover field and we let Bambi loose there...got up and the first thing we did was look out the window and again he was still there, ah.

But then he became a size that became dangerous. He used to try to follow the children to school. So I'd keep him home with a bottle of milk but there he was watching for them and then when he heard them at recess he went to school and he started to play and now he had hooves and he was this tall (three feet) and he'd jump about like a dog would and that was dangerous so, now he was big enough Bill had to build a crate to bring him back to the lake, and in the winter we'd come up with food for him and call him and he'd come. But there were (hydro) pole cutters up here and he hung around the camp and so anyway, we no longer saw Bambi.

But about seven years later, I was up there and some hunters came into the store and here's me making conversation — I certainly didn't approve of the hunting but, you know: "How did you guys do today?" And he (one hunter) said 'We didn't get anything but we had this deer follow us and it ate cookies, it drank a bottle of coke." And they said it was a seven pointer. We assumed this was Bambi. So at Christmas the men sent me pictures they had taken feeding Bambi — it had to be Bambi — and imagine these hunters (up there) to shoot (deer) and he follows them into the truck. But that was so nice because hunters wouldn't want to shoot such a small animal. If they're out there for food, they're not going to shoot a little runt. Thank goodness." ■

Dawn Goss

● Violet Ploshynsky (right) with her sister and pet dog.

PAM, Clear Lake 23

Wars come and go but fishing has always formed a big part of life in the highland lake country. For Merv and Shirley Neely, life at Wellman Lake usually included dropping a line in the water. "We had the fishing hole right out front in the bay here," says Shirley. "When we first came here — no trouble getting your limit." But that has changed over the years. "Now it's harder to get them, but there's jack, and northern pike and walleye. Even arctic char in nearby Glad Lake. Head down to Wally's Store at East Blue Lake and a Polaroid slapped on the wall shows off the record rainbow trout at 14 1/2 pounds." But for Merv, there's nothing better than "pickerel, or walleye — clean 'em, throw 'em in the pan, little bit of butter...yeah."

Merv Neely's first expedition to Wellman Lake was right around the end of the war. The only battles he would have were with the mud and the mosquitoes but it was enough:

"It was mostly people from Minitonas who started coming up here to Wellman Lake...We had what they used to call a 'Bennett Buggy' — with two Percherons, there was room in the back so we'd throw the boat in and all our gear. I was 15 when I came up...we got stuck in different places getting up here (so I) tried a short cut...got stuck...had to undo the horses and bring them around and of course they'd be right up to their armpits...you could hardly see them...We tented and of course the mosquitoes were a little thick but there was no trouble catching fish — just all kinds of pickerel and we were going out (to head home) and we just get across this bridge and it fell in — the back went down, and the guy hits the horses and they pull us out. It was ten years before I came back again."

The Old Campground at Clear Lake has attracted an eclectic mixture of summer residents ever since the park opened.

71

Dawn Goss

● Greeting a new day at one of Clear Lake's campgrounds.

THERE'S A CONVIVIAL COMMOTION ECHOING across the southern shore of Clear Lake — a happy chattering that's been rising from the 525 cabin lots that weave together at the Old Campground.

In this tightly packed summer community that sits in the achingly sweet surroundings of Riding Mountain National Park, there's a collective experience, a communal philosophy that's born partly out of park restrictions and partly out of pleasure — the pleasure of each other's company.

"It's the sense of small town," the campers will tell you. "Everybody knows everybody and once you've been here, you get hooked on the place."

So for a long time now the Old Campground has been attracting all walks of life, different ages, different professions and financial classes. Like the first people who came for thousands of years before, the early twentieth century brought campers lugging tents, and eventually trailers, lean-tos and make-shift huts. But it was all temporary, park policy insisting they were up and out each year by fall.

By 1978 park officials would allow cabins to remain all year — the people in them May to October. But in an attempt to maintain the natural integrity of the surroundings, they laid down rules about what you could and couldn't dig, or cut down or build. So for now, each lot is roughly 25 feet x 40 feet, the cabins are limited to a size no greater than 16 feet x 24 feet. They have hydro but no plumbing (there are communal washrooms and cold water tapes in the alleys), and permanent foundations are out of the question.

"Everybody knows everybody and once you've been here, you get hooked on the place."

Perhaps it is this air of temporariness that doesn't allow the cabin owners to make too much of the idea of ownership. Perhaps it is this lack of personal convenience that has led to a more communal lifestyle, conducive to a sense of community and an affirmation of the old message — less is more.

Scuba divers from around the Prairies are attracted to the deep, clear waters of East Blue Lake in the Duck Mountains.

Dawn Goss

We Are All Lake People

BY DUNCAN THORNTON

● Duncan Thornton prepares for another hike.

Although I was born and raised in Manitoba, I didn't grow up at the lake. Because my father came from Belfast and my mother was a Mennonite farm-girl, we weren't "lake people", not even camping people. We were more "go to the farm and help the cousins feed hogs" people.

But my wife did grow up camping and going to the lake. So when we got married, we were the third generation in her family to have our honeymoon at Wasagaming, the town at Clear Lake in Riding Mountain National Park.

Of course my wife didn't come with a cottage. Cottages at Clear Lake aren't easy to come by — it is a national park after all — unless you're left one in a will, which won't be happening to us. So we had our honeymoon in a hotel and it was great. Like any resort town, there's something relaxing about just being at Clear Lake — people have gathered there from all over to do nothing. Almost everybody is on holiday. There's swimming and trails to hike, and golf and tennis if you like that sort of thing, and there's just walking around. It's like Banff that way, though the hills and the prices are smaller.

In the last few years, as I have slowly learned the ways of my wife's people, we have shifted to camping at the park, at a particularly secluded spot we ask for by number. It turns out camping is an even more relaxing way of being at the lake, because idleness, just living, involves so many practicalities — cooking, keeping warm, walking to the bathroom — that any theoretical productivity could only be measured in negative numbers.

This is a camping day: we wake up early, because Clear Lake is high up on the Manitoba Escarpment and it gets chilly at night. I make a fire because I learned how in Wolf Cubs, and then I make coffee and scrambled eggs on the Coleman stove, and by the time we're done breakfast, the sun is getting warm and we get dressed properly. Dressed properly means sun-hats, walking sticks — ready for an expedition.

Then — and this is the great part — we walk through the bush and along a trail, and in twenty minutes we're sitting in town at White's Bakery (est. 1935). Now we have coffee someone else has made, and eat some excellent cinnamon buns. *Then* we're ready to get going.

Sometimes getting going just means poking around the shops. I would almost say that Wasagaming has too many quaint craft shops, but if it rains all day there's no such thing and you're pretty glad there's a log-cabin movie theatre too. A lot of the town's buildings are built like log cabins, many of them put up in the 1930s when it was the site of a depression work-camp that needed things to do.

Other times we get going on one of the trails. There are some good ones right by the town — the Ominnik Marsh trail takes you on a floating boardwalk through the marsh, with interpretive signs explaining what's around you. If you have a memory like mine, that's just as fascinating every year, and there are places to sit and wait for birds. And you don't have to be much of a woodsman to spot the beaver lodges and trails.

Some of the trails are a bit of a drive, and a bit of a hike, like Gorge Creek ("TRAIL DIFFICULTY: difficult," the trail guide says). Gorge Creek cuts deep through the bedrock of the Manitoba Escarpment, and you climb hundreds of feet through several different ecosystems. When you look east across the plains on a clear day, you can see as far as Lake Manitoba.

I'm told Riding Mountain has the greatest variety of animal life of any park in North America. It has the highest concentration of black bears, though we've been lucky enough never to meet one. We probably make too much noise.

But, of course, for us, the heart of Riding Mountain is Clear Lake itself, which is clear, and wide, and deep. We took a boat tour of the lake one year and our guide said he and a friend used to spend summer afternoons first hitting dozens of golf balls into the lake, and then putting on their flippers and masks and retrieving them so they could start over. Not really productive, but of course that was the point.

Last year I satisfied a modest but long-held ambition, and (after breakfast at White's), we set out to walk *all the way around the lake*. This isn't a particularly heroic thing, but it's an all-day hike, an eight-hour walk — out of the town, around the south end of the lake and through the Clear Lake Reserve (in 1930, in what might be Parks Canada's single worst moment, the reserve's inhabitants were removed to clear up space for the new national park, but they have returned, like anyone would). After the reserve land, there's the long north shore, where it can get mucky. I know because at one point I sank up to my thighs in mud.

By the time we got back to our camp, we were filthy and sore and miserable. So it's a darned good thing there are hot showers at the campsite. And it's a darned good thing we could then walk slowly into town, sit down at a restaurant where we had reservations, and drink wine and eat a big steak dinner.

Just a few days before I sat down to write this, we were there again, at our secluded campsite. It was on our last night there that I realized my family would go back to Clear Lake forever. My wife and I had stayed up late, until the campground was asleep, until the stars were bright in the cold still air, until the last of our firewood had begun to burn down. But my wife suggested a walk.

So we went through the bush, and along the lakeshore and down to the end of the quay. It was black and misty, and our breath hung in the air. The moon sat low in the southwest, and in the north, beyond the jagged silhouette of spruce and jack pine, the northern lights were rising. The lights shifted slowly up high and mirrored in the lake below, and then a star shot a farewell across the sky.

We are all lake people. ∎

So ask them why it is they come to this concentrate of cabins, this minuscule patch of earth with next-to-no living space and barely a yard, let alone parking space, to give up almost any sense of privacy, to haul their water from a cold-water spout outside, to get up in the middle of the night and walk down the street in their pajamas just to use the biffy, and they'll answer: "Because everyone else is here."

And folks here will tell you how the old cook shacks are the heart and soul of the place — all 31 of these park issue log frame kitchenettes that pop up in regular beats throughout the rear alleys of the place, with wafts of smoke and white spruce sap and an overpowering aroma that says "Hey, supper's ready."

They'll tell you how life around the cook stoves here is like a religion that you're born into — the older members teaching the younger ones how to light the stove (and how you light it with the fire in the front not the back so it heats the whole works). Or the campground telegraph that provides up to the minute information like: "Did you know there's synchronized swimming in the hot tub down the street," or "Hey, did you hear about that poor dog that got hit by lightning?"

The Biggest Log Theatre
in North America

BY DAWN GOSS

When the horizon leans toward dusk and the Wasagaming townsite is framed with a spruce whiskered moon, the stars shine on the marquee at Clear Lake's famous Park Theatre. But "The Show" is more than just theatrics for the happy confusion of cottagers who come out for the smell of popcorn after a long day at the beach, the buttery glow of theatre lights spilling over line-ups of hand-holding sweethearts, neighbours and friends. It's tradition, and one that hasn't changed much since 1937 when the building first opened.

Although the Park Theatre was one of countless cinemas appearing in Canadian towns during the '20s and '30s, what made The Park unique in Manitoba was its saddle-notched, horizontal log construction, a design to suit the architectural motif of the national parks at the time.

In establishing a private business in a park townsite, the theatre was subject to the approval of the parks branch. During the 1930s the degree of regulation increased particularly in the area of building design approval. By the time the Park Theatre was completed, the Architectural Division was directly involved in the preparation of plans for a wide range of private structures in an effort to promote a consistent architectural standard in the townsite.

Like Riding Mountain's Interpretive Centre, the Park Theatre's construction was modeled on Scandinavian methods in which the bottom of each log was scribed and hand cut to fit exactly over the top of the log underneath. Local craftsmen funded by federal emergency relief — cash aimed at generating employment in the national parks during the Depression — fell, peeled and manoeuvred logs to create the structure. At 71 feet x 116 feet, The Park would become the largest all-log theatre in North America. In 1995, it was designated a Heritage building by the Manitoba government.

"The only thing it wasn't built for was heating," says Bev Gowler, who along with her husband Jim, has owned the place since 1976. But considering that the 500-seat theatre is only open from the May long weekend to mid-September, the Gowlers don't have all that much to worry about. "Well, maybe on those few nights when you can't see the show for your own breath," laughs Bev, "but then we're probably the only place that hands out warm blankets to their guests." ▪

Clear Lake's Park Theatre has provided entertainment for summer residents since 1937.

Dawn Gross

So here we are on one of those crystal clear evenings when voices carry themselves up from the water's edge and the sound of wind chimes from the cabin two doors down. Here we are on one of those evenings when your bug juice has somehow gotten mixed up with the licorice you've been chewing, but that's okay because this has been one of those rare summer days and the air has more natural perfume than is bottleable and the people have gathered and the music is starting.

The infamous Clear Lake Eye Patch Band is warming up to a tradition that started 26 years ago when a guy name Don and his friend Ron and his friend Don and his brother Ron donned eye patches like Rooster Cogburn in *True Grit* and started marching around the campground and making music. It's been a summer tradition since, save the eye patches. You see, Don and the guys have been friends here for a long time and so have their wives and families. Their parents had cabins here — all pretty much 50 paces from each other.

Don Number One is strung to a temperamental one-sided bass drum that's been known to leap up off his belly on the occasional downbeat. The rest of the guys — well, let's just say there's a snare drum and a washboard and an accordion that slides into action, which in turn sends a group of middle-aged women out dancing in their night gowns, and the crowd grows bigger and they march to the left and they march to the right, and the bass drum marches into the biffy and blasts all the people out.

"Here we are on one of those evenings when your bug juice has somehow gotten mixed up with the licorice you've been chewing..."

"It's a long way to Tipperaaaaaaaarrrrrrrie!" they sing and the parade marches on. And so the music carries up and fades away, lost in all the twitters and tooters of man and beast. It blends with another season of wood stove smoke and white spruce sap and the quiet voice from the next cook shack that says: "Hey, where'd everybody go?"

Food always tastes better when it is cooked in the great outdoors.

OF COURSE, NOT ALL COTTAGERS RESIDE in the parks. Rob Wrightson and his family prefer to cottage in a reconstructed log cabin near the Crawford area just outside of Riding Mountain National Park. Rob says a lot of their outdoor life revolves around cooking. "We love camping...because you get up and you cook this really big, luscious breakfast and you go for a little walk and you come back and you cook again and you go fishing and you come back and you cook this huge evening meal and then you have lunch again before you go to bed, and you're sitting around the fire and if the mosquitoes don't drive you away then you decide oh, how about a smokie or a little bit of toast — bed lunch."

But the all-time favourite was one of the first times they baked bread on the wood fire: "You know how fresh bread smells, but out in the Riding Mountain backwoods by the water...you lift off the lid and you get that aroma of fresh baked bread and...uhhhh!...But I think that was the same weekend the bear came and knocked the tent down — guess he thought it smelled good too."

In the late 1980s a study was done on bear movements in and around Riding Mountain and it concluded that virtually all the bears within the park are influenced by unnatural factors, be it garbage dumps or the lure of abnormal food

Dawn Gross

It may not be a real mountain, but standing on the escarpment near Riding Mountain provides a breathtaking view of the Prairies stretching all the way to Winnipeg.

Dawn Gross

Sunset over William Lake in the Turtle Mountains.

ecosystems within the park boundary — accessible human food and garbage is certainly one of the causes of this nuisance bear business. To further protect the natural state of the area, a study group in the park is recommending changes to Clear Lake — getting rid of sea-doos and two-cycle engines, putting a limit on horsepower. Currently the park superintendent is intending to conduct more public studies before a final decision is made on the future of these vehicles.

But it's not the first time this old bone has been picked — the argument between those who want more development for recreational or industrial pursuits and those who want their summer sanctuaries to return to an even more wilderness state. The challenge is to plan development in a way that protects the characteristics that make cottage country attractive in the first place — the fundamental essence of the natural wilderness as haven. In 1977, the Wasagaming Master Plan was instituted in order to control and direct growth in Wasagaming. A focus of controversy, it took several years of public debate to finalize. By 1998, there was a set number of 256 cottage lots, 520 cabin lots and 510 camping sites.

sources. The park managed to move its dump to a less accessible area but cottage communities in other areas are still creating "nuisance bears."

Dealing with the welfare of bears is only one of many challenges faced by people coming to the lake. John Whitaker, chair of the Riding Mountain Biosphere Committee argues that allowing bears

to come in contact with unnatural food sources affects the naturalness of the bear population, which in turn affects the park's ecological integrity mandate of preservation and protection. According to a recent study — the report of the panel on ecological integrity — there are external threats to the park being able to maintain natural

Dawn Goss

BY JIM SHILLIDAY

Mother was looking forward to this day — July 31, 1988. Many times, in the last couple of years, she had smiled and said: "When I go to the lake…" Mary Ethel had had a good life and, in failing health, she looked forward to peace.

All the Shillidays, and the people they had married, and their children, were at the lake Mother had looked forward to "going to." We were spreading her ashes in Shilliday Lake.

Shilliday Lake is a small body of water up in the higher reaches of Manitoba, left over from the melting of a glacial sea thousands of years ago. It nestles in the Duck Mountains between and below West Blue Lake and East Blue Lake, latitude 51 degrees, 35 minutes and longitude 100 degrees, 56 minutes, not too far from Dauphin. Its deepest spot is 15 metres and it is stocked with sparkling, lively rainbow trout.

Mother had visited the lake several times, and was eager to spend eternity there because it was a lasting symbol of her boy, my brother, Robert Charles Shilliday. Her "Bobby" was just 19 when, as a Flight Sergeant air gunner, he was shot down while manning the mid-upper turret in a RCAF Lancaster bomber in a raid over Germany in the dying stages of the Second World War. His body was never recovered. Like so many thousands of Canadian mothers, she had said little about, but mourned much, his death.

For 33 years she had nothing honouring his memory but a Silver Cross sent to her by the federal government, and some old photographs and letters. Then, in 1978, she learned that a Manitoba lake had been named after her son by the Canadian Permanent Committee on Geographical Names.

Shilliday Lake is the lake Mother visited, and dearly wanted to be. Nothing represented her wishes more than these few words written by Christina Rossetti, who died one year before Bobby's mother was born:

> When I am dead, my dearest,
> Sing no sad songs for me;
> Plant thou no roses at my head,
> Nor shady cypress tree:
> Be the green grass above me
> With showers and dewdrops wet;
> And if thou wilt, remember,
> And if thou wilt, forget.

Shilliday Lake is a great place to fish, to relax, to enjoy a picnic. It is also a timeless landmark that makes sure these two people will never be forgotten. ▥

● A gentle path through tamarack and pine winds its way down to the shore of Shilliday Lake.

A Mountain Lake
of Our Own

BY DAWN GOSS

Brian Milne

At 4:30 on a Friday afternoon, our VW van is loaded almost to the ceiling. Luna, our border collie, sits straight up on the box between the driver and the passenger seats — ears forward, eyes bright. We're gassed up and geared up and heading north to our lakeside cabin.

If we're lucky, the traffic will be good — that is to say Rex, the neighbours' golden lab, won't be blocking the end of the lane, Popps' beef cows won't be hogging the right of way, and the strong aroma coming from Whitakers' coffeepot won't force us to pull off the road.

After we've battled the dogs and cows and coffeepots of Riding Mountain (or Hilltop) we'll be there. You see, "the cabin" is just three miles up the road from our house, and we're driving in an area where getting away from it all means not having to go all that far.

We found our land quite unexpectedly in 1988 while on the way to photograph at nearby Riding Mountain National Park. We stopped to follow the trail of some Black Eyed Susans when we stumbled on a section of bush for sale and in it, 40 acres of gorgeous living water — perfectly alive with ducks and geese. "You're not buying that slough?" queried the woman behind the counter at the Erickson town office. Not long after it was ours, and we were delighted.

Next, we found our 12-foot by 20-foot clapboard cabin at Ken's Antiques in Neepawa. Ken, a gregarious, bowler-hatted, bulbous-nosed, 80-something antique guru, could usually be found in a doorway vigil, set up in his comfy chair or at a farmyard auction, ready to "pump pump organ" at a moment's notice. With a wee bit of bargaining, a fist full of cash and a signature smooch that left nose tracks across my glasses, the deal was sealed. But what good was our new cabin in his yard?

In a land where it is not unheard of to see a towering grain elevator rolling down the road, moving this two-roomed "baby" seemed like nothing at all. In fact this was the second time it had hit the road, having had a former life with a bachelor in Franklin (about 10 minutes west of Neepawa). Climbing 1,000 feet up the mountain was a little slow, but not a problem, neither was dodging a few hydro lines. In fact, the cabin looked quite pretty moving across the horizon, its blue paint set nicely against the wild roses blooming in the ditch. It was the last 3/4 mile (better known as the 'Driveway from Hell') that proved to be the problem. The semi driver hauling our load took one look at the tiny laneway through the bush and, not wanting to scratch his new cab, promptly left, leaving trailer and cabin at the edge of the road and us with the question: how do you get a 12-foot cabin down a 7-foot-wide driveway?

Enter one John Deere 4050 tractor and the 'Hilltop Society of Friends and Neighbours'. We dragged and heaved and pulled through poplar bluffs and open meadows right on down to a nice sheltering line of spruce trees, close to the water but out of the wind.

If you flung open the cabin now, you'd see, aside from a few pieces of wood furniture, white —

all white. "Don't you think the place could use a little colour" popped out one neighbour. "Nope" I said. The fact is we prefer it white and plain and simple, it relieves our eyes and draws them closer to the living pictures, the simple, ever-changing landscapes that appear to us through each of the five windows.

We heat our coffee on a spiffy little second-hand wood stove that we use to heat the cabin, or on a propane stove set up on the washstand outside. If we're really energetic, we'll light up our $15 cook stove. The cook stove dons a cat-in-the-hat style stove pipe that plays a tune when the wind blows just right. An old jam kettle makes a good substitute for a bathtub, particularly now that it's become a summer ritual and no matter how many parts we can or can't fit into it.

Inspired by a never ending quest for a little "society", we organize friendly cross-country ski weekends, quinje overnighters, and baked-bean breakfasts buried in the snow. Warmer weather brings evening campfires, with overall-clad neighbours sprawled out on the ground like wolf kill. And in pure prairie summer tradition, garden parties have become an annual event, drawing a potluck of coquettishly costumed friends from miles around.

We have never officially named the cabin. It's just "cabin", the lake just "lake" and the land "land" —

The Northern Lights illuminate the night sky above the Goss/Milne cabin.

all we know is that it's there...and when time allows us, so are we.

When an out-of-province acquaintance declared, "Well, it's not exactly what I'd call cottage country!" I bit my lip. He'd never really know this place — there's not enough time for him to see its value. It's not what you'd call in-your-face postcard glorious, but it gives quietly in small surprises that sneak up on you and then are gone: the fleeting squeak of the 13-stripe ground squirrel that pops up beside the log at the campfire spot; the smooth, powerful swoosh of the pelicans flying 10 feet over your head; the family of screech owls that surrounds you in the garden, or the great grey that lands on the roof of your car; the Northern Lights as they dance on all four horizons, angels winging up to the centre of the sky, hissing and crackling out their shapes and colours; your nephew lying back in the tall grass, watching the world float by in the clouds and saying, "You know, I really like it here."

The wind's picking up the trees behind me and cutting a stream of ripples through the otherwise glass-like lake, glowing golden in the evening light. The cool air off the water carries a small but happy muttering of kids laughing in the distance, which in turn sets off a short howl of coyotes to the north. I have another cup of coffee. Its essence rises up and mixes with the sweet smell of black poplar and sage, of water and earth.

It's peaceful here, I think I'll stick around. ▪

Brian Milne

Brian Linehan

A Texas fisherman, desperate for a picture to show his friends back home, "borrowed" this Lake of the Prairies pike from the little boy in the boat who actually caught it.

To the north, the development issue is being felt on a different but no less passionate scale. Recently, the provincial government changed the boundaries of Duck Mountain Provincial Park to accommodate a forest leasing agreement with the Louisiana Pacific Lumber Company. Despite the Clean Environment Commission (and others) urging that all resource extraction be phased out of the provincial park, the province is allowing more logging in what it insists on calling a "natural park".

"There was quite a history of logging here," according to Boris Hryhorczuk, whose father had a saw mill at Cash Lake, "but it was selective logging...that's very much different than what's being done at the moment...that's where you can really draw a contrast — how they used to do it and what the hell is going on now."

The issue for Duck Mountain, as it is in the rest of the province, is one of intelligent planning. How much extraction or development can each lake area sustain from an environmental and aesthetic perspective. For Riding Mountain, as a national park, the mandate is clear — protection and preservation. The superintendent is obligated to ensure that. For other areas — the Ducks, the Turtles and the Lake of the Prairies district — the coin is still up in the air.

ABOUT 12 YEARS AGO BRIAN MILNE and I bought a section of land a few miles from the southeastern border of Riding Mountain National Park. It's a lovely mix of poplar and spruce forest, open meadows and beavered creeks, and in the centre, a small lake.

The idea that we were reverting what had been zoned and posted as 77 deeded lots back to conservation land didn't sit well with some neighbours who thought we were "working against progress." But the individual lots had not been selling and the idea of 20 docks and motor boats lining the delicate shoreline of this quiet, hidden landscape didn't seem quite right to us.

We moved one small cabin onto the place — plunked it about 100 metres from the water's edge. Most of the time we walk in. And we've had our battles with stray hunters and ATV's and ski-doo's and people wanting to log the joint. But it's worth it.

It's worth it just to hear the quiet — the wind gently tossing the tree tops, spitting up a little spray in the middle of the lake; water bugs etching out the ripples along the reeds; the odd lynx, or elk or bear moving through.

It's been a privilege, and we hope that for a long time more than the loons will be laughing on our little piece of paradise. ■

WHERE PRAIRIE MEETS
ROCK & WATER

The Whiteshell Region

BY C. J. CONWAY

The Whiteshell. Aboriginal people called the white shells they found there *megis*, and thought them important agents in the creation of humans. The Great Spirits, according to legend, literally blew life into the first inert human forms with this sacred shell. I've never found any of these, but I'm told they can be spotted in the park still. It was a good choice to name the area.

WHEN EXAMINING THE WHITESHELL, one single thing asserts itself again and again. This place is a land of change. Where prairie meets rock and water. Where the boreal forest, lying like a dense carpet across northern Canada, embraces the last vestigial tip of southern forests. All the animals and plants of these diverse zones can be found in this lovely interface too, from cactus to oak to jack pine, from white-tailed deer and raccoons to moose and wolf.

The Whiteshell is also a place of convergence. Natives knew this. Explorers and fur traders would learn it too. Early settlers figured it out the hard way, and it is the thing people like most about the place now. The white pines grow up like sentinels along the shores of the lakes, and meadowlarks, birds from the grasslands, sing their flutey song for whomever is lucky enough to hear. Some of the lakes are pure Shield country, rocky shored and clear and deep. Within close distance, the same rivers that supply those lakes often look like prairie streams, with abundant soil banks and large leafy deciduous trees that overhang the slow, turbid waters.

In order to get a picture of the place, I will describe parts of the wildlife, lakes, rivers and people of the Whiteshell. In doing so, we will come to know this place a little better, and like a great painting, enjoy it more the closer it is examined.

The Whiteshell is a place of convergence. Natives knew this. Explorers and fur traders would learn it too.

USUALLY DESCRIPTIONS OF PLACES in Canada start out with what is known about the first people who lived there, the indigenous tribes. Unfortunately, the records we have of earlier people date back only as far as the first white people who visited and kept notes. Certainly, archeology and known tribal settlement patterns tell us more, but for the most part, our notions are based on the experiences and impressions of the first explorers.

In this case, the intrepid Frenchman La Vérendrye paddled up the Winnipeg River from Lake of the Woods and met Cree at a place he called La Barriere. He gave it this name because the

natives were trapping sturgeon in a weir. This site is very close by what is presently Opapiskaw campground. The Cree would gather every year here in large groups, perhaps several hundred, and process great numbers of this immense, oily fish for winter consumption. The flesh was boiled, the oil scooped off and stored in birchbark tubes. The meat was pounded into powder, which later could be mixed with wild rice, dried berries, and re-hydrated with the stored oil. La Vérendrye, a veteran of Napoleonic wars, and the first white man to explore the far west, came through the Whiteshell in the early 1730s.

Many others would follow, but even at the time of La Vérendrye's inaugural visit, there were ancient petroforms adorning parts of the Whiteshell. These rock arrangements stymie archeologists, because without organic material, carbon dating techniques cannot be used. Fortunately, an ancient village was discovered near one of the sites, where human-made materials were excavated that date as far back as 500 A.D. It is sheer interpretation to assume the petroform rock formations are the same age, but something about these outlines, some 25 metres across, suggest that they are older than our clumsy tribal nomenclature. Some take on the appearance of snakes and turtles, as well as more complicated shapes, which may have had special religious significance. The snakes and turtles are near portages and trails, while the larger, more vague renderings are off the traditional pathways.

La Vérendrye would be back, and the Winnipeg River would be in use for more than a hundred years as a major fur trade route. This marked an important change, since prior trading had been done south from Hudson Bay. For many years the canoes passing through the Whiteshell would be coming from Montreal, funded by the North West Company. The natives would never be the same again. And although the brightly dressed voyageurs no longer ply the waters, sing chansons or smoke their pipes, Highway 44 is named The Vérendrye Trail in remembrance of this first explorer.

After the colourful years of the North West Company were over and the more staid managers of the Hudson's Bay Company ran Canada's fur trade business as a monopoly, there was a rare

Aboriginal petroforms, which held religious significance for the Cree and Ojibway, can be found along remote waterways of the Whiteshell.

opportunity for an artist to visit this huge tract of wilderness. Paul Kane, a young painter from Toronto, caught a ride with one of the fur trade brigades and sketched his way across the Wild West in canoes, on horseback, dog sleighs, York boats and on foot. One of the sketches he would later make into an oil painting was of an 1846 encampment along the Winnipeg River, which he describes in his journal as an endless series of rapids, all with French names and some small enough to be run without portage. In his painting the smooth rock shores, with the occasional boulder, produced a first glimpse for the world of what the Whiteshell must have looked like then. Trade goods like knives, axes and guns littered the bottom of these rapids from earlier capsizings, he said, easily visible, but unobtainable because of the dangerous current.

The fishing that was done by natives and remarked on by La Vérendrye continued to interest anyone who came to the area. Early pioneers used it to supplement their diet, and it attracted Piscean enthusiasts almost from the beginning. Native fish like sturgeon, northern pike and walleye were later supplemented by stocked fish like bass and trout to create a world-class fishery.

PAM, Caddy Lake 1

THE FIRST WHITE PEOPLE TO STAY in the Whiteshell area were brought here by an entirely different lure. Searching for gold was an affliction caught by many of the navvies employed during the Canadian Pacific Railway's construction. After all, they had dynamite, knew the basics about minerals, and most importantly, were working in areas that had never before been checked over by prospectors. A few of these men would make the trek from rail construction sites and penetrate what must have been then the darkest reaches of wilderness. Some would find gold, but all would have the kind of adventures that caught the public's fancy, as stories from the Klondike were published and sold around the world.

From a camp on the shores of Star Lake, two men were living the same life. We love to hear about those times still, and luckily, they were written down. Just as important, it was the early infrastructure of trails and knowledge these men developed and described that would make it possible for others to come later.

⬤ Early road access allowed nature lovers to explore previously unreachable areas of the Whiteshell.

Harry McFie and Sam Kilburn were interested in looking for gold, but stories of their times in the park at the turn of the century is treasure for the ages. In order to survive, the men trapped, fished and traded with local natives. To get to their place they departed the train at Ingolf, and paddled down Long Pine Lake. They would have portaged into West Hawk, one of two lakes named for an earlier prospector, and make another short hop-over into Star. Most of their travel would be done in canoes, or on snowshoes in the winter. Once Harry walked to Falcon Lake, named for Pierre Falcon, a Métis of some stature during his life. Not only did Falcon write a song that voyageurs adopted as one of their paddling favourites, but later he would serve as a magistrate of the District of White Horse Plains, the locus of the buffalo meat-hunting business, which the Métis developed to supply the fur trade with its staple, pemmican. Falcon wrote scores of songs about his life and its strains, but unfortunately, most are lost to us. Perhaps Harry was on his way to meet one of Pierre's family while hiking miles to pick up the present day equivalent of a Woods Five Star sleeping bag. It weighed just seven pounds,

Poet Rupert Brooke.

Harry bragged, and would keep him warm on the coldest nights. It was a blanket made out of plaited rabbit skins, and apparently a highly valued item. Over time Harry and Sam would own a dog team, reducing winter walking and increasing their range from home.

Errors in judgement could be more costly than skinned shins and lost time. McFie's book tells of a man who got his feet wet walking along slushy-iced lakes, with severe frostbite the result. Realizing the trouble he was in, the man broke into an abandoned cabin on West Hawk, near the portage to Long Pine. He was unable to start a fire, and after no one answered his emergency gunshots, turned the weapon on himself. Deadman's Point is named for this poor anonymous wretch.

At some point the area must have become too crowded or dull for our wilderness adventure seekers, because they were off to new frontiers and adventures like Alaska and the First World War. The prospecting they did before they left must have been promising though, because a mining operation was developed at Star Lake, the Penniac

Reef Gold Mine, that operated right until the outbreak of the Great War. A more lasting legacy is McFie Lake, in the park, and Kilburn Lake, farther up the English River system.

Rupert Brooke referred to Winnipeg as "hideous…even more hideous than Toronto or Montreal."

One of the first tourists to the Whiteshell was the famous English poet Rupert Brooke. He toured Canada in 1913 and, according to his journals and letters, was singularly unimpressed with our cities. He referred to Winnipeg as "hideous…even more hideous than Toronto or Montreal." Brooke had a different impression, however, of the wilderness area now known as Whiteshell. Along with a Winnipeg friend, he visited George Lake, not far from Pointe du Bois. For several days he swam, canoed, fished and explored the remote lake, pronouncing it "wonderfully and incredibly romantic." Brooke returned to Europe and was killed two years later during the Great War.

They Called Him **Alfie**

BY BRIAN JOHNSEN

One of the grandest sights in the Whiteshell is a honking flock of wild geese winging over the cottage. Most of these geese are heading for a specific location — a sanctuary nestled on the Rennie River. The refuge was founded by Alfred Arthur Hole, a mink rancher who homesteaded just south of present day Highway 44.

Alf Hole was both an avid outdoorsman and a natural character. His life changed in 1937 when a railway worker appeared at his door with four orphaned goslings found hiding between the ties of the CPR mainline. The worker bet him a 40-ounce bottle of rye whisky that he couldn't raise his new brood to six weeks of age. Rising early every morning, Alfie would feed them hand-picked dandelions. That first summer the goslings ran free in the barnyard and, after obtaining a permit from the Canadian Wildlife Service, Hole clipped their wings and wintered them with his chickens. The following summer, Hole single-handedly built a rock and earthen dam across the Rennie River to create a pond for his gaggle, the first of many he was to construct over the years. He successfully mated the lone female with an old gander and she laid and hatched four eggs. After they were branded, they were set free on the lake.

In the fall, his young geese heard the calling of the wild as thousands of their untamed cousins flocked southward. But the following spring Alf's geese returned. For the next eight years the irascible but kindly Hole worked ceaselessly on his sanctuary, building several more dams and making the area safe for his progeny. In the evening Hole and his little black dog would walk to the place he called "his office," the Rennie Hotel, where he would purchase two beer — one for himself and one for his dog. For almost 20 years he kept his flock. But in 1957 the aging Alfred Hole sold the property to the Manitoba Game Branch.

Alfred Arthur Hole died on December 23, 1959. For 60 years the geese have returned each spring to the sanctuary named in his honour. ∎

Guy Fontaine

BY THE EARLY 1900s, THE LAKES of what is now the Whiteshell were getting busier. Homesteaders were moving in. The Dominion Lands Policy promised 160 acre parcels of Crown Land for the price of ten dollars. The property was granted on the condition that the pioneer build a house and begin cultivating within three years. Many were granted in the Whiteshell, the choicest property being closest to the railways. Samuel and Mary Corbett homesteaded on West Hawk from the 1880s until about 1926. They lived off the land, and were supplemented by a remittance cheque Sam received once a year. They went to Kenora for the absolute necessities, until a store opened at Ingolf around 1923. Their plot was nearly 20 acres and never paid for, rendering them squatters. They raised chickens and had a garden, but little else is known about these two. He was well educated, and receiving a remittance annually from England was not unusual among early English settlers. Apparently, Mr. Corbett lay about all day writing poetry while Mary did the work, even rowing him around in a boat. We can only speculate why he and his family had decided he should leave the comforts of home to start a life in the Canadian wilderness.

There were quite a few pioneering families trying to make a go of things in the Whiteshell during the early part of the century. Many were Scandinavian, and even Sam McFie, with his Scots' name, claimed Swedish as his mother tongue. It was marginal farmland at best, however, and over time many would move on to greener pastures or more urban existences. Their tenure would shape settlement patterns to come through the construction of roads and trails to help get themselves and agricultural products to railhead.

The Canadian Pacific's line pushed through the muskeg, lakes and rock first, with the initial train travelling to Winnipeg from Kenora in 1882.

The park's early development was focused around the construction of the railways. The Canadian Pacific's line pushed through the muskeg, lakes and rock first, with the initial train travelling to Winnipeg from Kenora in 1882. The last spike in this cross-country link was pounded in 1885, the same year Louis Riel swung from a gallows in Regina.

PAM

In 1947, 35 people died when the Camper's Special train, returning from cottage country, crashed into an oncoming locomotive near Dugald.

The End of the Line

BY ELLEN PETERSON

The train line has always run through the heart of our lake community near the Ontario border. In this corner of the Whiteshell, there is a cluster of lakes named for the wives of early trainmen: Florence, Marion, Nora, Eveline. A few settlers took homesteads in the area long ago, but the settlement we know today as Florence Lake began as an Arctic Ice Company logging camp. When logging operations were discontinued in the 1920s, a few of the employees returned to use the old camp buildings as summer homes and the rest, as they say, is history.

Since the beginning, the summer residents counted on the train for everything. It was the only way to get to the lake, and the only way to bring in supplies. You thought twice, maybe three times, before bringing in lumber or a piece of furniture. If you forgot to bring it, you borrowed it from somebody or did without. If the stove needed repair, you learned to fix it yourself rather than face the ordeal of taking it to the city for repair or bringing in a new one. Everything had to be shipped in by freight, lifted off the boxcar, carried down a steep slope to the dock, loaded onto a boat and, in the early days, rowed across the lake to the cabin.

But that was in the 1940s and '50s — the heyday of Canadian train service, with at least one train everyday, and a great little weekend train called the Camper's Special that left the city at 5:50 p.m. on Fridays and got back to town at about 10:00 p.m. Sunday nights. The *Winnipeg Tribune* was brought in and delivered to your door by a couple of local youths in a rowboat. Mail was picked up and delivered twice each week. You mailed your grocery order to Eaton's and they would box it up and send it down. In emergencies, you were lucky if one of the resident doctors was at his cottage to stitch a cut or pull a fishbone from a throat. The only other recourse was to go across to the station, call the Dispatcher on the callbox, and put a stop on the next train through.

A shared passion for the natural world, as well as our dependence on the trains and each other, forged a loving and cohesive community. Many of the cottages were built in the 1930s and '40s, and some are now housing a fifth generation. The very proper mothers of the early years, worried about the effects a summer in the wilds would have on their youngsters, instituted a Sunday night hymn service. A box of hymnbooks and a piano were freighted in and rowed across, and each Sunday evening at sunset the community gathered to sing hymns: *Onward Christian Soldiers, Marching to Zion, Abide With Me*. At intermission, the youngest children present passed the plate, but the plate was full of candy, and no donation was expected. "Sing Songs" are still held occasionally, and many of us know the words to a remarkable number of hymns. Call out the number of a hymn, and someone is sure to say "Oh, that was Mrs. So-and-so's favourite." Mrs. So-and-so departed this world fifty years ago, perhaps, but I am sure she can still hear Number 681 floating out across the quiet water.

Most of the socializing happened at the station. Friday nights especially, everyone would gather to meet the Camper's Special and catch up on the news. All summer places have their own folklore: stories of chance meetings with bears or rare birds, rumours of the biggest fish or the best berry patch. We formed firm friendships with the conductors, and could tell by listening if the approaching train was a passenger train or a freight. Many romances bloomed on walks along the tracks, and intermarriages have united most of the cottagers as families-in-law, as well as in spirit. Generations of children have pressed pennies on the rails and carved their initials into the station building, a practice that continues today, though the trains are few and far between.

Time seemed to stand still at our lake for many years, without roads, electricity, or telephones. But nothing lasts forever, and by the 1980s, outboards had long replaced the rowboats, and you could occasionally hear a cell phone ringing. The *Winnipeg Tribune* was gone, Eaton's was gasping its last, and train service wasn't what it used to be.

Instead of regular service, our lifeline — the train — now ran only a few times a week. And they ran late, often ran three, five, seven hours late. The price of a train ticket skyrocketed, making a family vacation too expensive for many. Concerted efforts to lobby for improved service were unsuccessful. We struggled along as best we could, experimenting with other ways to get to there. You could drive to Nutimik and charter a plane. You could drive to Caddy Lake and walk for five hours on the Mantario Hiking Trail: a beautiful experience but not for the faint of heart. You could get Wayne at Caddy Lake to drive you in his "Water Taxi" down to the end of South Cross Lake and walk just two hours on the tracks.

The railway finally ceased even its freight service to our stop, making it impossible to bring in enough supplies for a holiday. After lengthy debate, careful study and no little regret, it was decided that a road was the only solution.

Our new road runs 13 kilometres through the forest, and is the result of many hours of hard work. Every effort was made to minimize the road's impact on the environment, neighbouring communities, and on our own way of life. It is a beautiful drive, and the parking lot at the end is hidden from view so that when you stand on your dock, the modern world still seems pretty far away. There are gates and locks to keep our private road private.

Although we are glad to be able to get to the lake with ease, we miss our Friday nights at the

The author enjoys a paddle on Florence Lake.

station, waiting for loved ones and friends. We will need to learn new ways to keep our lake family tightly knit. The First Annual Tailgate Party was held on August 14, 1999, to celebrate the opening of the road. The youngest children at that party will have no memory of the time before the road, but they will have their own harrowing adventures, their own wonderful stories of long ago in a place far from the city world. They will know the words to a few hymns, and they will be blessed, like their forebears, with a true spiritual home in the wilderness. ■

The stories and lasting influence of this construction are all around the park today. Caddy Lake, named for a CPR engineer, used to be called Cross Lake, and the fill required to carry a rail roadbed cut the lake in two. A tunnel was blasted through later. All the work was done with horses, dynamite and muscle. The bottomless swamps and hard, heavy granite assured the financial demise of several contractors. Underestimating the work and not paid until completion, many of the short spans, given out to small contractors on bid, had two or three different companies attempt to finish them satisfactorily. It would have been heartbreaking to have been advanced the last credit possible, with men unpaid, and not quite be able to pick up payment. This happened more than once along the CPR's line between Winnipeg and Kenora.

A tiny settlement carries the name of another engineer, John Rennie. The son of a famous English engineer, he was knighted after the completion of his father's proposal to build London Bridge.

● Many of the improvements made to the Whiteshell Provincial Park were provided by Depression-era unemployed living in nearby work camps.

P.A.M., N17858

Whiteshell UFO Scare

BY DOUGLAS ALLEN

Everyone has a scary lake story – the ones they tell on those wild nights when it's dark and the cottage gets lit up by lightning every 15 seconds. The best ones are about the possibility that we're not alone.

Steve Michalak's tale is one of the best stories in the Whiteshell. Steve went mano-a-mano with an alien spacecraft. He claims to have actually touched one. The date was May 20, 1967, and Steve was prospecting for gold, just north of Falcon Lake. Swatting his way through the bush, he found a promising vein of quartz. While inspecting his find, Steve heard a sudden trumpeting of geese. He looked up and saw two "cigar shaped objects" hovering in the sky just ahead. They were glowing red, and slowly descending. One stopped, but the other landed on a flat rock, not 100 metres in front of him. The second craft then took off and disappeared.

For the next half an hour, Steve made a sketch of the craft. Suddenly a door on the side of the craft opened. Steve approached to about 10 metres, and heard "human-like voices" coming from inside.

Convinced that this was some secret military vehicle, Steve boldly walked up to it, thinking that they were having "engine trouble." He tried several greetings in different languages, including Russian, to no avail. Steve looked inside and saw a panel of lights, some of them flashing. Stepping back, he began examining the craft. It appeared to be made of a stainless steel-like material. Deciding to risk it, he reached out and touched the side. Fortunately, he was wearing gloves because the metal burned his hand. Before he could react, the craft suddenly shifted position. He now found himself facing a vent of some sort, and before he knew it, he was hit by a blast of hot air. His shirt and undershirt caught fire. The craft then took off and disappeared. Steve began to feel extremely nauseous and developed a severe headache.

Somehow Steve managed to get back to Falcon Lake and returned to Winnipeg the next day. He had phoned his wife and told her he'd had an "accident." In Winnipeg, he was taken to the hospital. Soon afterwards he went public with his story and officials launched an investigation. A visit to the site found radiation levels so high that the government cordoned off the site.

Investigators eventually categorized the vehicle as being "of unknown origin." Yet Steve had a series of "spots" on his torso that defied medical explanation. A good case for Scully and Mulder and a great tale for a midnight bonfire. ■

UFO victim Steve Michalak displays the results of his encounter with a "cigar shaped object."

In Their Own Words:
Big Whiteshell Lake

BY YUDE HENTELEFF (AS TOLD TO MARY JANE MACLENNAN)

Yude Henteleff is a well-known Winnipeg lawyer and long-time summer resident of the Whiteshell.

"I was about 19 years old when my Uncle Harry scouted Big Whiteshell Lake to build his cottage. We pitched a tent and brought our fishing rods along, and we were catching five-pound pickerel like we didn't know what to do with all of them. It was such a rich, rich lake at that point. At any event, we scouted it and found our lot.

The road from Rennie to Big Whiteshell was about the worst road you could ever travel and we had to haul everything in. And of course there was no power. So everything had to be carried in, and everything had to be done by hand labour and over a period of three summers.

In the evening you could hear wolves howling across the lake, and moose would come right up on the shore. On one occasion a female moose with two babies climbed up on the shore and walked right by us. It was an exquisitely beautiful place; it still is, but in those days there were only a dozen cottages.

The cottage was really a labour of love. We just gloried in it, and friends came and helped and all the rest of it. The work never stopped. But it was

● Yude Henteleff at Big Whiteshell Lake.

enormously relaxing and the children would be as much help as they could. The neighbours were also very helpful. I mentioned Mr. DeCagney. He lived right next door to us. Remarkable man. He was blind. It was the Dirty Thirties, and he and his friends would come and camp at Big Whiteshell and literally live off the land.

Well, he knew every inch of that lake, even though he was blind. And he and I would go out fishing and he'd say, "Okay, Yude. What kind of a wind is there? What direction is it coming from? How sunny is it? How cloudy? Okay, just go to the particular place."

We'd get to the place and he'd say, "Which way are the waves coming?" and he'd go through the whole thing again, and he'd say, "Well, stay about 20 yards out and go about this speed." There must have been 15 boats around. Nobody was catching fish, but pretty soon we were just hauling them in. He knew every hole, he knew every place and he had a million stories. It was wonderful having neighbours like that.

The Aboriginal people used to come every fall to gather rice. In those days the women still wore traditional clothes, had the babies strapped on their backs. It was like a scene out of the early eighteenth century. And they actually gathered the rice and cooked it right there in big pots to get ready for shelling. In those days they used their paddles to batter the ripe grain into the canoes.

Sometimes we'd put our four kids in the boat, plus the two of us and our dog and go all the way to the falls, all the way to Lone Island. The first time we saw those falls, we just couldn't get over the beauty of it. And in those days also it was inevitable that you'd see moose along the river, browsing on the shoots. We'd pick blueberries, strawberries, and raspberries by the tonne. And in some places wild plums we could make into jelly, so the land gave so much delight and joy.

Nowadays you have governments that clear-cut in a provincial park. It's very destructive to the environment and they leave a façade, a screen of 30 or 40 feet so people can't see it from the road. When you see the destruction, it's really terribly sad. I hope they'll see the light of day and see that what we have a sacred trust. Future generations deserve a chance to enjoy the cottage too." ■

The Canadian National built their line about 25 years later, the two lines crossing each other near Rennie. The motive power of the day required wood or coal, and water was taken on several times for a steam engine between Winnipeg and Minaki, or Winnipeg and Kenora, on the CN and CP respectively. These requirements, along with plenty of routine maintenance work after initial construction, provided part and full-time employment for many of the homesteaders along the rail line. Families would look after farms while the man of the house earned some ready cash.

The railway also provided a means for people to get to remote places on a regular basis. Early cottaging stems from this fact. People from what had been unthinkable long distances could be whisked to lake country with speed and style. Many people coming to look for their own piece of paradise were employed by the railway and travelled for free. Ingolf was originally populated by summer campers and cottagers who mainly worked for the CPR and travelled on a pass. Old railroaders talk of the requirement of setting a boxcar full of beer into a small siding at Ingolf for Saturday night dances.

Trying out a new water-skiing device at Falcon Lake, circa 1952.

IT WAS IN 1920 THAT THE PARK REALLY started to grow. The general economic health of the era and the proximity of lakes to the railway combined to make Brereton, the Nora and Florence Lakes area and West Hawk-Falcon the places people first started cottaging in the Whiteshell. Once the federal government finally handed over the resources of the land to individual western provinces, Manitoba was free to set up forest reserves where it saw fit. In 1931 the Whiteshell was named as a reserve.

At the same time a road was being built that would link Whitemouth and Rennie, travel past West Hawk and on to the Manitoba-Ontario border. This is known today as Highway 44, but was then part of the Trans-Canada Highway. The road we think of now as the Trans-Canada was not built until 1955. It was the construction of the original highway that brought cottagers to every lake they could drive to, and explains why Highway 44 is still important for water access, if not cross-Canada travel.

Much of the roadwork, and most of the public buildings and campgrounds were built by workers housed in the Unemployment Relief Camps. Few countries were affected as severely as Canada by the worldwide depression of the 1930s. One in five Canadians became reliant upon government relief for survival. The western provinces were technically bankrupt from 1932 onwards. At this point Prime Minister Bennett sanctioned the creation of a nationwide system of camps to house and provide work for single, unemployed, homeless Canadian males. Occupants voluntarily entered the camps and were free to leave at any time. In return for a bunkhouse residence, work clothes, medical care, three meals and 20 cents per day, the men worked 44 hours a week. Hundreds of these men toiled in what was then the Whiteshell Forest Reserve. Miles of hand-laid rock-retaining walls leave a lasting reminder of their efforts.

These symbols of human labour — railway construction and relief camp projects — stand in blunt contrast against efforts to lessen man's burdens. Hydro-electric projects and nuclear power research are also part of the Whiteshell's story. In 1911 Winnipeg City Council decided to build its first hydro-electric plant at Pointe du Bois on the Winnipeg River. Today, six generating

Julius and Goliath

BY DOUGLAS ALLEN

One of the realities of cottage life is learning to live with bears. The Whiteshell provides ideal habitat for black bears, and a large population roams freely throughout the region. By nature, black bears are usually pretty easy-going, and tend to avoid humans. However, they are subject to mood swings, and with their size and strength are capable of inflicting serious damage to both property, and life and limb. As such, relations between bears and cottagers exist in a kind of détente.

Conventional wisdom has is that the most dangerous situation is encountering a mother and her cubs. Yet the vast majority of human encounters with bears centre around food. Driven by the biological imperative of their hibernation lifestyle, bears have a voracious appetite. When it comes to food, which to a bear is virtually anything, they adopt a "what's yours is mine" attitude, and brook no dissent in this regard. Simply put, being between a bear and something to eat is not a good place to be, and refusing to surrender even a peanut is folly.

While mainly vegetarians, bears are also opportunistic carnivores, and will not hesitate to go after a meat dish, particularly if it appears to be weak, or defenseless. This puts young children at risk, and is a constant source of anxiety for all parents. For the Rosenberg family of West Hawk Lake, this anxiety became a nightmare on September 20, 1992, when a bear attacked their two pre-schoolers.

Julius, aged five, and his three-year-old sister Barbara were sitting on the dock having a snack. In accordance with standard procedure for children of their age, both had on their life jackets. Which was fortunate because suddenly a bear appeared on the dock, and started coming toward them. They jumped into the lake, but the bear followed them and quickly overtook the two youngsters. It seized Barbara by the back of her life jacket. Julius grabbed her from the front, and a tug-of-war ensued. Julius began yelling at the bear to let go. He finally wrenched her loose, and they paddled frantically back to the dock.

They started to run for the cottage, but the bear had swum to shore, and was now blocking their way. Julius resumed yelling, and even began to growl at the bear, who, no doubt confused, eventually backed away enough for the children to get to the cottage. Denise, their mother, had heard the commotion, and was coming to investigate. She opened the door, Julius and Barbara ran in, and she closed it in the bear's face.

For the next few minutes the bear wandered back and forth peering in the windows, before finally slouching off. Denise called the RCMP, who showed up minutes later to find the bear relaxing on the dock eating the children's snack. Under the circumstances, the bear was shot.

Julius later said that he was worried about his sister, and anyway, he wasn't afraid of bears! He was awarded the Governor General's Award for Bravery. ■

Tom Thomson

stations harness almost all of the river's 106 metre drop.

Since 1965 the Winnipeg River's water has also been used as organic coolant at the Whiteshell Nuclear Research Establishment. At its peak, the research centre was home to about 1,000 scientists, engineers and support staff. An early project was the development of a forty mega-watt reactor. Later efforts focused on the storage of radioactive nuclear waste.

Pinawa's finest hour probably came during the crisis known as Operation Morning Light. Early in the morning on January 24, 1978, a Soviet satellite accidentally re-entered the earth's atmosphere over northern Canada. The concern was that the reactor core that powered the space craft was out there somewhere in our Arctic, an incredible hazard if it were. The Soviets claimed that the reactor core had burned up while hurtling towards earth, and for the most part, they were right. However, tiny pieces of radioactive material were showing up everywhere. The most dangerous, a piece about the size of a nickel, was found on the ice covering Great Slave Lake. Eventually over 4,000 of these particles would be

Tom Thomson

● West Hawk Lake remains popular with both cottage-owners and daytrippers.

Whiteshell lakes are home to a wide variety of fish, some stocked —
like trout and bass, and some indigenous — like walleye and northern pike.

Tom Thomson

gathered up and brought back to Pinawa for testing and storage. The USSR made a payment of three million dollars to help pay for the search and safe-keeping of another of their nuclear goof-ups.

The Whiteshell has a powerful association with things falling out of the sky. West Hawk Lake, the deepest in Manitoba, was formed by a meteorite. Falcon Lake is 21.5 metres deep and Caddy 5.8, but West Hawk is about 110 metres deep. In 1965 two Canadian astronomers undertook a project to drill a hole deep below the bottom of the lake to look for evidence to prove the meteorite theory. The test drill bored 727 metres. Near the 450 metre mark, micro fractures in quartz crystals started to show up. These are consistent with findings in test drills at places like the Barringer crater in Arizona. Scientists estimate West Hawk was formed by a meteorite 150 metres in diameter. When it hit the earth they believe it was moving at 58,000 kilometres per hour. It blew a hole almost two kilometres in diameter through solid rock deeper than the Richardson building is tall. Imagine the sound on impact!

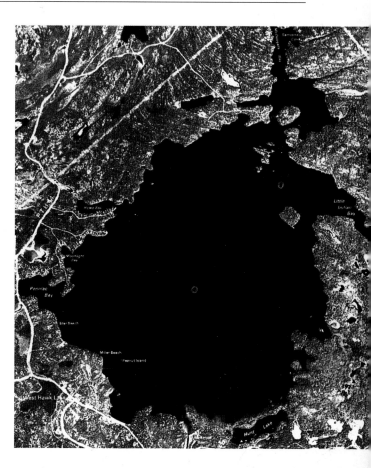

West Hawk Lake is the end result of a meteorite crash during prehistoric times.

Dave Reede

ALONG WITH SIMPLE NATURAL BEAUTY, it was probably stories of the incredible fishing that brought the first summer campers, and later cottagers to the Whiteshell. An active angler can catch almost every native species of central Canada, and even a few exotics that have been introduced. Lake trout favour deep cool-watered lakes like West Hawk, since they have the highest oxygen requirements, and carp, which seem to be able to complete their life cycle in ditches, are in the park too. Choice game fish like walleye and northern pike exist in record sizes and goodly numbers. Locals call these same fish pickerel and jack, but whatever the name, they taste great in a pan. The sturgeon, once so plentiful, have a tougher time now. Dams and other habitat changes, as well as their slow reproductive habits and earlier heavy harvests for their roe, the prized caviar, has put this dinosaur of the deep into a nearly extinct category. One or two leviathans are still snagged every year by unsuspecting anglers, and the image of a mossy-backed, armour-plated six-foot long sea-monster rising up beside a small tin boat is one that likely gets taken to the grave.

Enjoying the end of a long day at a remote cottage on Big Whiteshell Lake.

Dave Reede

You Remember Every Canoe Trip

BY BILL REDEKOP

Y ou remember every canoe trip. In a short period I have canoed the Whitemouth River in mid-August when it was a rock garden and we didn't know better; Long Lake, Garner Lake, Francis Lake, the Souris River where my dear departed friend Dan Leskiw discovered buffalo bones from an early Indian campsite; the Manigotagan River just days before I was to wed (they really do seem like rivers of life); the Winnipeg River system where we met a lone Viet Nam vet from Winnipeg's North End and heard his harrowing tale around a campfire one night; the Red River, Roseau River, and the chain of lakes on the Whiteshell River starting with Caddy Lake.

These trips maybe were nothing special compared to the voyageurs of old but the rivers and lakes wind through my memory whenever I look at a map of Manitoba.

The Berens River paddle was special. The Berens is an early fur-trade route. It was also the site of famous research by American anthropologist A. Irving Hallowell in the 1930s on early Ojibway beliefs, including windigos, thunderbirds, medicine men, and shaking tents.

Our plane landed in an early June drizzle and we loaded our canoe the next morning in dense fog. The innkeeper said it reminded him of the heavy mist

the day of the fatal Sowind airplane crash in 1997, killing four people and seriously injuring 13. But the mist lifted almost as soon as we touched water, like a good omen, opening to a picture-perfect blue sky.

I'm not at all superstitious. I doubt God would leave little signposts around for us to read, like a novel. So on our first day, when we found two perfect moose jaw bones laid on the shoreline like an offering, I thought they'd make a great souvenir and took them. We then proceeded to get hopelessly lost, winding up in a channel barely the width of our canoe, and blocked by a mammoth beaver dam. Rethinking superstitions and retracing our route, I returned the moose bones.

The Berens is a magnificent river. It's in the Canadian Shield but the cliffs are higher than further south: the moss is thicker, and the jack pine struggle

The author takes a well-deserved break while canoeing the Winnipeg River.

harder to survive. We traversed 47 rapids, shot about half and portaged the rest. The portages are relatively short, which is why the fur traders liked the river.

But the weather turned unseasonably cold on us. One day we paddled for hours through falling snow. We woke up another morning to find our tents iced up. We hadn't brought warm clothing, or warm sleeping bags. Other times it rained, or we paddled into stiff head winds. By the fourth day, my friend Syd said I really shouldn't have disturbed the moose bones. We came across other animal skulls placed on rock cliffs or along portage trails but chose to ignore them.

On the sixth day, we saw what looked like a human skull in some rapids. We tried to get a closer look but the rapids whisked us away. Was it the mind's temptation for superstition, after a lengthy time in the bush? This occurred at Lower Conjuring Falls. A conjurer is another name for medicine man.

On our first portage after Conjuring Falls, I sprained my ankle. It was a severe sprain and I could no longer walk, never mind carry packs or the canoe.

Fortunately, we were near the end of our trip, where the Berens empties into giant Lake Winnipeg, and by evening found an old logging road beside the river. Two men out for a drive gave us a 15 kilometre ride into Berens River First Nation.

I was doing a travel piece for the *Winnipeg Free Press* and wanted to interview some elders. I hobbled around to interviews on crutches obtained from the nursing station. People in Berens told me about evil spells laid by conjurers. I learned people still go to conjurers to lay a hex on an enemy. Or someone would suspect an enemy had laid a hex on them. I learned hexes are cast mainly out of jealousy. There is a surprising amount of jealousy on some reserves.

Elder Percy Berens of Berens River First Nation told me about the battle between thunderbirds and giant snakes. Thunderbirds produce lightning when they open their eyes. The bolts are often aimed at giant snakes the size of balsam firs. Percy believes these beasts still exist, and said someone had recently found wing feathers from a thunderbird.

He told me stories about windigos — cannibalistic monsters that live in the forest — and giant moose and giant frogs and even giant mosquitoes that once existed.

I told Percy I loved the stories but I couldn't believe them. They sounded like Greek myths, I said. He is a worldly man and understood the comparison.

We then returned to our everyday lives in Winnipeg. But a year later in the reception room of my chiropractor — a bone doctor? another coincidence? — I came across an article in *Canadian Geographic*. It said 10,000 years ago the beavers were as big as bears, a ground sloth was the size of an ox, and the bears were as tall as a moose. Evolution, mainly the competition for food, caused wildlife to shrink over time.

I laid the magazine down and stared ahead. I wanted to tell Percy. Then again, I guess he already knew. ■

Chilling Out at West Hawk

BY STEVEN SCHIPPER

I spent some of my teens lamenting my ill-timed birth. If only I'd been born a few years earlier, I could have experienced free love, and hitchhiked to Woodstock, and harboured draft dodgers. Instead I was sandwiched between the psychedelic era and the "me" generation, torn between idealism and ambition. No wonder I wrote in my high-school yearbook, "The one materialistic thing I want in life is a summer cottage by a lake."

My parents were never able to afford a cottage. In fact, they had to show their T4s to my summer camp so I could get one of the few scholarships handed out each year. Camp was where I first fell in love with lakes, those great pools of water surrounded by rugged terrain and primitive buildings. I grew to love the cool rocks beneath my bare feet, the wind in the trees, the lapping of waves against the dock, the smell of woodsmoke and wild roses.

It might as well have been a different country, so far removed was the lake from my home in Montreal. There, I lived in a neighbourhood where you were lucky when there were no smells, and where the streetlights made the stars almost disappear. It was a great city, and I liked it enough to study there after graduation. The National Theatre School attracted the finest young talent from across the country, which is how I fell in love with a Winnipeg girl. She was beautiful, gifted, and charming, and I swear I fell in love with her before I knew her parents had a cottage at West Hawk Lake.

I remember seeing it for the first time: the shady green yard, the lake shimmering in the sun, the modest cabin lined with warm, knotty pine. The next thing I noticed, being a young man in love, was how far my room was from my future wife's. But love, like water, finds the route of least resistance, and a day came when everyone else had gone back to the city. The leaves were turning by then, and the lake was still, and the wooden deck was rough against our skin. If I hadn't already loved her, heart and soul, her parents' cottage would have sold me on the idea of spending the rest of my life with her.

So it is that almost everything I love, I owe to my late in-laws. These days, my wife has picked up her father's tools and become quite handy, taking care of things around the cottage, and shooing me out the door each morning. She knows I have another great love, besides her and the children and the theatre and the cottage. The Falcon Lake Golf Course is only fifteen minutes away, and it's a bit of a miracle: a championship course, open to the public.

Sometimes I stroll down the fairway and remember the young man who wanted to be a hippie. I wonder what he would think of my playing such an establishment sport with such joy. In the jargon of his day, he'd probably freak out. Then I'd show him the loving wife and children, the cottage, and that lake, and he'd chill, man. He'd just chill. ∎

Smallmouth bass are not native to the waters of the Whiteshell. These fish were chucked out of rolling boxcar aquariums into track-side lakes during the early 1900s, the on-board biologists conducting crude experiments in fish stocking. Despite the methods, the hardy fish has thrived. Struggling up rapids and creeks, it now inhabits almost all the lakes in the Whiteshell. The few it does not are the direct result of more bio-tinkering. Rotenone was used to poison all the fish in Hunt, Lyons, Camp and Burton Lakes. The chemical was applied right at ice-out, in the late 1940s, so that more exotic fish could be put in their stead.

Brook, brown and rainbow trout, along with splake, have been plopped into these lakes with varying degrees of success. A survey done in 1988 showed that perch and bullhead had infiltrated the trout stocks. It is not known if these fish gained access naturally, were being used as bait and escaped, or in the perch's case, perhaps weren't successfully exterminated in the first place. Bullhead are not native to the Whiteshell. As well,

Burton Lake has a small member of the bass family known as the pumpkin seed living in its waters now. This is another fish that has come to the park as an uninvited guest. How long they stay or how many of them will eventually visit is difficult to say. To make good on the area's reputation as a great fishery, let it be known that a sturgeon weighing 275 pounds was caught in the park. The province's largest ever perch, a two and a half pounder, was snagged here too.

For a few lucky souls, this desire was addressed by parents or even grandparents, and a cottage at the lake has been part of life for as long as they can remember.

THE WHITESHELL HAS MANY SITES like this that make it more than just a park. The museum at Nutimik is a fabulous place to check out many of the artifacts of the early settlers and homesteaders. It includes opportunities to learn about the natives who lived here and describes their lives, pastimes and methods for survival in this beautiful setting. But what the park provides more than anything is a chance for urban people to escape the stress and strain of everyday life and relax along the shores of one of the many lakes contained here. Whether it is a weekend trip to a campground or the trek to the cottage, something in all of us needs to get away. For a few lucky souls, this desire was addressed by parents or even grandparents, and a cottage at the lake has been part of life for as long as they can remember.

One place that seems to embody this notion as well as any is the Law's place on Falcon Lake. Long before the highways were built, Gil Law decided he wanted to visit Falcon Lake. He and his friends would pack up knapsacks with bare essentials, a few cooking utensils, some food, a hatchet, matches and tea and caught the train to Ingolf. Once there, they would get in a canoe and paddle the length of Long Pine Lake.

Once they made the kilometre-long portage into West Hawk, it was another paddle, this one farther than Long Pine, about four kilometres. The journey was far from done. There were short portages from West Hawk into Lyons and Camp Lake. No groomed trails, they were slugging it out through bushy ground to get to Falcon Lake, which because of its remoteness had a nearly untouched fishery for the young men to enjoy. At the end of a weekend or holiday the journey was reversed.

Mr. Law liked Falcon and decided to build a cabin in a sheltered bay at the east end of the lake. With the help of family and friends, trees were cut near the site of the future cabin and dragged to the lot for peeling and construction. As much as possible, they used on-site material. Anything else would have to be hauled over portages, and that prospect led to plenty of ingenuity. All the furniture was fashioned by hand, for example. Despite that, many things had to be brought in on their backs. Some items were too heavy for one man and poles were made to suspend the weight between two or more hardy portagers. The fireplace was built of stones from the shoreline. A log icehouse was constructed and the men came out in the winter to cut refrigerant blocks for the summer to follow. The original cook stove, which weighed 500 pounds, was brought out by truck along the old Dawson trail to East Braintree and from there to the west end of Falcon Lake.

In this era of microwave ovens and e-mail, the Law's cabin still does not have road access, electricity or telephone. A propane hot plate and fridge are grudging concessions to the modern age, and the trip to Falcon is by car now, where it is parked and the remainder of the journey completed by powerboat. Although this represents a huge change from the first days, there remains at this isolated and idyllic place a very clear sense of what attracted families like the Laws to cottaging in the first place.

SUMMER COTTAGING, AS WITH many great traditions, changes to reflect the tastes and limits of the time. There are too many of us now to have lakes to ourselves, and not many would go to the effort the first cottagers in the Whiteshell did. At its worst, modern camping can seem like we have moved the suburbs to the woods, but it is, nonetheless, a force that drives us. 'Going to the lake,' is one of the things that makes us Canadians. We all want a place to visit on the hot lazy days, somewhere to escape the demands of daily life, to be closer to nature, to work on projects that only expert tradesmen would be allowed to tackle at home, to be near the water and to feel that we could survive if we had to.

We all want a place of peace and quiet in the woods — a place with rickety old wooden chairs, screened verandahs, peeled logs, and a glimpse of water through the trees. For a hundred years, this is the grand tradition that has been celebrated in the Whiteshell. With all the amenities, points of interest and beautiful lakes, I am sure there will be people heading to the Whiteshell to summer along its shores for another hundred years yet. ■

Tom Thomson

ESCAPING TO
ONTARIO

The Lake of the Woods/
Minaki Region

BY JAKE MACDONALD

I n 1957 my parents purchased a small piece of cottage property on the shores of Lake Lulu, a hundred miles east of Winnipeg in Northwestern Ontario. With seven kids to raise, they were already busy enough. But they seemed to think it was important to have a summer place. So my mother took charge of the endless rustic chores — laundry, cooking and cleaning — while my father built the cottage with his own hands. Thanks to them, my siblings and I came to know the uniquely Canadian experience of "going down to the lake", and that experience, without a doubt, shaped us all into the people we are today.

A young Jake MacDonald proudly displays his first big fish.

OUR LITTLE PIECE OF PARADISE was officially known as "Lake Lulu" on the map. But everybody called it "Laclu," a French name that we adopted without knowing its origin. Our property consisted of a one-acre parcel of hayfield that had once been a pasture for dairy cattle. There were no trees and the long grass was crawling with wood ticks. It wasn't an ideal cottage site, in other words. But my father got busy planting a variety of hardwood saplings and we got busy having fun. The hayfield, once cut, made a fabulous playing field for British Bulldog and plastic baseball. And the lake was narrow enough — about half a mile across — that we'd swim across it and back on a dare.

The Laclu Road was a winding seven mile-long gravel track that led out to the Trans-Canada Highway. During the summer, my dad worked in the city while my mother and the kids stayed at the lake. It was an idyllic life. We constructed tree forts, hunted gophers, portaged into neighbouring lakes, and swam all day long. On Friday night, we put on our shoes (shoes, no less!) and embarked on a long hike down the gravel road, planning to meet our father when he arrived from the city. There was always a great feeling of expectation as we hiked along, expecting at any moment to see his car appear in the distance. But if he was late — and who isn't late leaving the city on Friday night? — we'd begin to get excited as the miles passed beneath our feet. Was this going to be the night we set a new record? Four miles up the Laclu Road, there was a bridge across Lower Louise Creek. One night we made it all the way to the bridge before we saw my father's great white, shark-finned 1959 Buick come cruising over the hill.

Sometimes on Saturdays, we drove to Kenora to shop for groceries and get an ice cream. Kenora was only twenty minutes away, by car, so I've always considered it part of my psychic home territory. Kenora was a rougher town then. The waterfront was a fascinating jungle of seedy buildings, creaky wharves, and scummy water. My brother and I would sneak away from the family and explore the shady caverns beneath Chez le Rat, checking out the discarded liquor bottles and muttering bums. If my dad was in a good mood he'd award us with a rare treat — a tour on the old wooden cruise boat known as the *Argyle II*. The *Argyle* was the best way to see the Lake of the Woods. You could stand up on the prow with your hands on the wooden rail and watch the hundreds of verdant islands glide by. My dad was a serious reader, a passionate consumer of history books, and he'd tell us about the lake's history as we cruised along. One of his favourite characters was La Vérendrye, the French explorer who first mapped the Lake of the Woods.

My father always took satisfaction in pointing out the bigotry and unfairness that underpin our national histories — the outrageous falsehood, for example, that Canada is a nation of "two founding races." First of all, he maintained, the French and the English are not races. And Canada was not settled by Europeans. It was settled by Aboriginals. When La Vérendrye "discovered" the Lake of the Woods in 1732, it had already been populated for thousands of years. La Vérendrye knew a bit of Cree, and translated their place name "Min-es-tic," into "Lake of the Woods." Surveyors later determined that the correct translation from the Cree was in fact "Lake of the Islands". But by then, the great explorer's name for the lake had dried — just another little error that hardened into history.

Tom Thomson

Receding glaciers gouged the Canadian Shield, leaving behind the lake and river systems that we enjoy today.

LAKE OF THE WOODS IS FED from the south by the Rainy River, and is drained at the north end by the Winnipeg River. It's a young lake; with scars and rock rubble strewn like construction damage along its shoreline. As I got a little older, I read some history myself, and learned that the force that created this huge excavation was a mile-high wall of ice called the Wisconsin Glacier. About 12,000 years ago, the Wisconsin Glacier slowly bulldozed its way across most of contemporary Ontario. Twelve thousand years may seem like an enormous span of time to us, but really, it isn't. To put it in perspective, consider that an average human life lasts 72 years. In those terms, the Wisconsin Glacier melted off the land only 160 lives ago.

By 7,000 B.C. the glacier had completely disappeared, leaving the enormous Lake Agassiz, which in turn receded and left behind the Lake of the Woods. The Lake of the Woods would have eventually drained off to the sea (as did most of Lake Agassiz), but it was seated in one of Nature's most impervious bedrock formations — the Precambrian Shield. The Shield is composed of granitic rock, which doesn't absorb water. So the remnants of Lake Agassiz formed tens of thousands of lakes, the largest of which is the Lake of the Woods. It's impossible to discuss the Lake without describing the Shield itself — a slab of rock covering more than half of Canada. So let's go back even further than the Ice Age, for a moment, and consider the genesis of the Shield itself.

To put it in perspective, consider that an average human life lasts 72 years. In those terms, the Wisconsin Glacier melted off the land only 160 lives ago.

The age of the Precambrian Shield is almost beyond human comprehension. At 2.5 billion years, it makes the Himalaya Mountains (60 million years) look like mere toddlers. It covers every square foot of Labrador, 95 per cent of Quebec, 70 per cent of Ontario, 60 per cent of Manitoba, half of the Northwest Territories, more than a third of Saskatchewan, and a good chunk of northern Alberta — all in all, it's a piece of real estate larger than the Indian subcontinent.

"Precambrian" means that period of history before life emerged. During the Precambrian epoch, the Lake of the Woods district was an inhospitable place indeed — a wild land of erupting volcanoes and cataclysmic tectonic upheaval. The buckling crust of the earth formed towering mountains, right where the Lake of the Woods now lies. But four ice ages of approximately 100,000 years apiece reduced those mountains to the well-worn, smooth granite hills that surround the lake today.

When early European explorers arrived at the Shield, they encountered an endless, primordial, and unyielding wilderness. Many of them promptly drowned, starved, froze to death, or went bush crazy. The smarter ones noticed that the Indian inhabitants of the Shield survived not by harnessing the land, breaking it, bending it to their will, but by riding it as lightly as a bird rides the wind. The Indians built tools, clothing, vehicles and shelters out of the materials on hand — bark, skin, sinew, fur, feathers, balsam sap, grass, and wood. They owned little, and carried little on their backs, because everything they needed was all around them. It was far from a Hiawatha-like paradise, of course, and starvation often stalked native hunting bands during the latter days of winter. But in general, they fared much better than the first Europeans, who quickly learned a hard lesson — you do not conquer the Canadian Shield, you survive it, and then only if you are clever, light-footed, and resourceful.

Aboriginal people have been living on the Lake of the Woods for about 8,000 years. Oral histories don't go back that far, but the most likely scenario suggests that as the glaciers shrank, they entered the area to explore, perhaps hunting along the cliff-edges of ice. The region was populated by terrible and fabulous beasts, such as the wooly mammoth, the sabertooth tiger, the giant bison (the remains of which have been found around Kenora), and, greatest and most fearsome of all, the short-faced bear, which preyed on the huge bison. The short-faced bear was a nightmare from every Boy Scout's dreams. Weighing in at about 2,000 pounds, the short-faced bear (or "cave bear") stood about twelve feet tall on its hind legs. There are no records or written histories to suggest how the first humans dealt with this awful beast. But for certain, overnight camping trips in bear

● In order to survive, the first Europeans to arrive in northern Ontario learned to embrace Aboriginal lifestyles.

PAM

The White Pine

BY C. J. CONWAY

● Along with rock and water, the white pine is the dominant feature of the Northwestern Ontario landscape.

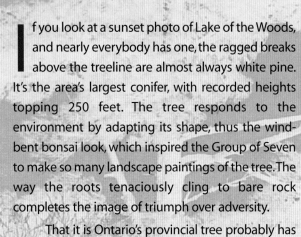

If you look at a sunset photo of Lake of the Woods, and nearly everybody has one, the ragged breaks above the treeline are almost always white pine. It's the area's largest conifer, with recorded heights topping 250 feet. The tree responds to the environment by adapting its shape, thus the wind-bent bonsai look, which inspired the Group of Seven to make so many landscape paintings of the tree. The way the roots tenaciously cling to bare rock completes the image of triumph over adversity.

That it is Ontario's provincial tree probably has a less arty origin. After the Baltic Sea was closed to the British by Napoleon, that great sea-faring race started looking farther afield for its shipbuilding timbers. At that time stands of white pine stretched from the eastern seaboard to the prairies. The frenzied logging of this tree went on for decades, and no less a founding father than Sir John A. Macdonald expressed concern over the tree's extinction, and Quetico Park (near Thunder Bay) was eventually set aside as a white pine timber reserve.

During the early years of Confederation, the monies collected in tariff through the white pine export business exceeded the entire cost of government. So in a sense, the white pine built our country. The tree built the country in a practical sense too. Canadians in the early 1900s were rocked in pine cradles, raised in pine houses and buried in pine coffins.

Young pines are accustomed to reproducing below a canopy of mature adults, and they have trouble competing with the faster growing replacement species that spring up after early logging. So it now has a "remnant" position in the forest, with just the occasional tree sticking out from stands of aspen or balsam. Foresters have probably done the tree the most damage, though. People who sought to grow large plantations of the valuable timber imported a disease to North America. Unwittingly, their efforts brought a plague that threatens to wipe the tree from our landscape.

The disease, first identified here in 1914, starts its life in currant bushes, then travels as an airborne spore, penetrating the needles of its secondary host. Once in the tree's needles, the disease creeps toward the trunk, eventually killing everything above that branch. Scientific efforts, ongoing since the disease's discovery, have failed to produce a consistently resistant seedling, or to curb the disease's spread once in the tree. Concerned tree-lovers might improve a white pine's chances by removing all currant bushes from around the tree and cutting off infected tree limbs as they appear. Efforts to replant the trees in disease-free areas are ongoing. And lake-dwellers can help the campaign by planting trees on their property, and tending them through their highly susceptible early years. ■

country must have sometimes produced appalling scenes of bravery and terror.

As the glaciers melted and the Lake of the Woods stabilized around its current shoreline, forests and grasslands became established. The climate became appreciably warmer (even warmer than now) and many ice-age animals died off. Some were perhaps hunted into extinction by those same Indians, who migrated into the area in greater numbers as the landscape became more lush and attractive. As the big plant-eaters died off, the big predators disappeared with them. They were replaced by scaled-down species that are still with us today — timber wolf, black bear, moose and beaver. The Lake of the Woods of that period was a comparatively easy place to make a living — full of fish, waterfowl, and enormous tracts of wild rice. In the sheltered forests the Aboriginal hunter-gatherers pitched their tents, cooked over their fires, and for most of the year, maintained a standard of life not much different from the idyllic sort enjoyed by canoe trippers today. The European philosopher Thomas Hobbes once opined that prehistoric people endured lives that were "nasty, brutish and short." It's worthwhile to

remember however, that approximately 12 million Aboriginal people somehow managed to survive in pre-historic North America — no small number, when you consider that even with the "benefits" of welfare and modern technology, only about one-tenth of that original population survives today.

It's hard to differentiate between the various Aboriginal groups who originally populated Lake of the Woods, but by approximately 500 B.C., the record becomes substantive enough to identify the tools and weapons of the so-called "Laurel Culture." The banks of the Rainy River contain a great number of Laurel burial mounds, which have offered up a treasure of artifacts, including skeletal remains. The bones in these burial sites are found in bundles, which suggests that decomposition had occurred before burial. Archeologists therefore speculate that Laurel natives conducted some form of religious rite when a member of the band died. Sometime around 1,000 A.D., the Laurel Culture vanished. The fate of these people is uncertain, but they may have been displaced or exterminated by the "Blackduck" people, who dominated the area for the next 700 years. The remnants of Blackduck

PAM

● Native women were the primary harvesters of wild rice — a staple of the Aboriginal diet.

In his search for the Great Western Sea, La Vérendrye depended upon the advice and experience of Aboriginal guides.

PAM

culture can be seen today in the rock paintings found in Lake of the Woods. One site is near Dead Man's Portage, and another is between Painted Rock Island and Split Rock Island near Sabaskong Bay.

Towards the end of the Blackduck era, other tribes moved into the area. When the first white traders arrived in the 1700s, the lake was populated mainly by groups of Cree and Assiniboine. The Ojibway (who dominate the area today) didn't arrive on the Lake of the Woods until around 1800. The Ojibway were an adaptable and innovative group, and they managed to live peaceably with the Cree and Assiniboine. The Sioux (or Dakota, as they are sometimes called) were not so easy to get along with. The Sioux lived on the south end of the lake, and there was constant tension, and, at times, open warfare between them and the northern tribes. Around the year 1800, the Cree migrated to northerly parts of Ontario. The Assiniboine moved west into Manitoba. And the Sioux abandoned their attempts to control the region, leaving the Lake of the Woods in the hands of the Ojibway.

It is generally agreed that the first white person to see Lake of the Woods, in 1688, was a young Frenchman by the name of Jacques De Noyon. While De Noyon's immediate interest was fur, like all the French explorers he dreamed of finding a route to the Pacific Ocean. But he probably went no further than the Lake of the Woods. In 1730, the Commander of a small trading post on Lake Nipigon was told of a great river that flowed west from Lake of the Woods, to a great sea. He was captivated by these tales, and literally began having dreams of discovering the fabled *Mere de la O'uest*. Eventually, he succeeded in convincing some Montreal merchants to finance him, and on June 5, 1731, he left to find the western sea. The dreamer's name was Pierre Gaultier de Varennes, Sieur de La Vérendrye.

La Vérendrye towers over the history of the Lake of the Woods like a great white pine. As a boy, La Vérendrye heard of the exploits of the early French explorers — Jolliet and Marquette, La Salle, and Radisson — and resolved to spend his life exploring the wilderness. While hustling sponsors for his explorations, La Vérendrye pretended to be interested in fast profits and trade opportunities.

But privately, he viewed those sponsorships as simply a means to keep his canoes pushing west. His lack of interest in finance surfaced in the normal way. And for most of his life, he had problems with large bills and small paycheques.

In the spring of 1732, after wintering at Fort Kaministikwia (Thunder Bay), La Vérendrye paddled out of the Rainy River into Lake of the Woods, accompanied by 50 birch-bark canoes manned by the best native troops he could muster. La Vérendrye's intention was to build a permanent settlement on Lake of the Woods, so the party made their way across Big Traverse to the inlet of the North West Angle. At the mouth of the inlet, he built a palisade and named it Fort St. Charles. The fort consisted of a timber stockade and several cabins made of logs and clay. With the completion of this rude structure, La Vérendrye and his men became the first white settlers on Lake of the Woods.

It might seem odd that he built his settlement at the shallow, southwestern corner of the Lake of the Woods. After all, it lies some distance from the outlet of the Winnipeg River, where his western journeys would begin and end. But the choice of locations was influenced by his local guides, who knew there were extensive wild rice beds in the area. If fur was the gold of La Vérendrye's day, wild rice was the silver. High in protein, it was a dietary staple and a tradable commodity. There was also abundant fish to vary a diet of rice, bannock, moose meat, and venison. During one of his outings, La Vérendrye and his men caught 4,000 whitefish, which they smoked for the winter. The land surrounding the Fort was fertile, so they planted wheat and had some success with their harvests. So the first years of the settlement were prosperous ones, despite the hardships imposed by the harsh winters.

For most of his life, La Vérendrye had problems with large bills and small paycheques.

From the very outset of his arrival, La Vérendrye kept an eye out for unfriendly neighbours. He was aware of hostilities between the Sioux and the other tribes. Isolated skirmishes had been escalating into larger battles, and rumours were rife that the Sioux were preparing a major assault. In late December, 1733, a large contingent of Assiniboine and Cree arrived at Lake of the Woods. Coincident with their arrival, word came that the Sioux had killed four Cree, and the air was strident with cries for revenge. La Vérendrye persuaded the Indians to postpone hostilities until the spring, but in exchange, had to promise to send his son with the war party. His anguish at this prospect is recorded in his journal, "If I refuse to let him go, I have reason to fear they will…come to the conclusion that the French are cowards." In the end, his eldest son, Jean Baptiste accompanied a force of 700 warriors into Sioux country, and although he survived, his presence may have sparked an episode of revenge, two years later.

In the summer of 1736, life at Fort St. Charles turned hard. The wild rice beds flooded, general provisions ran low, and supplies from the east never arrived. The gunpowder supplies at Fort St. Charles were dangerously low, and to make matters worse, the Sioux were becoming more aggressive. To bolster his supplies, La Vérendrye decided to send a party to Mackinac Island for provisions. Once again, he turned to his eldest son to lead the mission. Completing the party was a Jesuit priest, Father Aulneau, and nineteen others. They departed on June 5th, intent on rescuing the Fort from impending disaster. But they were never seen again.

Three weeks later their bodies were discovered. The killers were probably marauding Sioux, who intercepted the group by chance. La Vérendrye was heartbroken, but the danger remained so high that it wasn't until September that he dared slip out of the Fort and recover the remains of the victims, which he buried at Fort St. Charles. La Vérendrye wasn't precise in his description of the massacre site, and even now, there is some debate about the true location of the tragedy. Some hold that the island currently known as "Massacre Island" is not on the logical route the victims would have taken to get to the Rainy River. Others contend that when travelling east, the French used a route through Sabaskong Bay to get to Rainy Lake, thus avoiding the upstream paddle at the Rainy River. Short of new archeological evidence, it is unlikely the true location will ever be known. What remains however, are the eerie images that haunt the imagination when you visit the possible massacre sites.

The voyageurs enjoyed breaks based on the time it took to fill and smoke their small clay pipes.

In the early years of British dominion, the canoe routes to the interior fell into disuse. The trade in furs was conducted exclusively from Hudson Bay, although forays from the Bay posts did reach the Lake of the Woods area. Despite having to pay homage to a new King, the French did not abandon the industry they founded, and by the latter part of the 17th century the songs of the voyageurs rang throughout the forests. Eventually they united as the North West Company, sparking a fierce, and sometimes, bloody rivalry. However, this struggle for control of the fur trade proved too costly, and finally the two sides called an end to the rivalry, and in 1821 they merged under the banner of the Hudson's Bay Company.

Now in possession of two avenues of trade, the Hudson's Bay Company began to develop the water route from Rainy Lake to Lake Winnipeg. In 1836 the HBC built a post called Rat Portage House on an island at the outlet to the Winnipeg River. And in 1861, the company moved the post to the mainland. (This latter site eventually became the town of Kenora.) Initially, this development was strictly commercial in nature, undertaken for the sole purpose of facilitating the movement of goods associated with the fur trade. All this changed with the founding of the Red River Settlement. This tiny colony proved that a permanent agricultural community in the West was possible, despite its isolation from the rest of Canada. Assuming an importance far beyond its size, the colony at Red River became the key to the emerging western half of Canada.

Lake of the Woods Museum

Society ladies take afternoon tea on the deck of Kenora's Yacht Club.

Prime Minister John A. Macdonald sent an expeditionary force through the wilds of Northwestern Ontario in 1870 to quell the Riel uprising at Red River.

PAM, N5363

Winnipeg mayor W. Sanford Evans often visited the Yacht Club.

Royal Lake of the Woods
Yacht Club

BY C. J. CONWAY

The first summer cottages were built on the shores of Lake of the Woods as early as 1881 along Keewatin Beach Road. Motorboats were not in use until the late 1890s, so early campers had to rely on canoes, rowboats and sailboats. In any place where boats exist in number, it isn't long before people start arguing about whose is faster.

By 1903 a club was organized for racing both rowboats and sailboats. A year later, six separate classes of sailboats were competing, using the building that serves as today's clubhouse. This organization was a forerunner to the Royal Lake of the Woods Yacht Club, which became the cradle of competitive sailing in western Canada.

The Canadian Pacific Railway — which forged a connection between Winnipeg and the Lake of the Woods — also helped produce a number of millionaires, many of whom were Winnipeggers. The relationship between Winnipeg's economic health and the Royal Lake of the Woods Yacht Club was an important one. When the bloom came off Winnipeg's real estate boom in 1912, activities slowed at the Yacht Club as well. Still, when the Duke of Connaught and Princess Patricia visited western Canada before World War One, the Yacht Club was a stop on their tour. It was this sponsorship that conferred 'Royal' status to the club.

The outbreak of war ground things to a halt, and it wasn't until after the conflict that problems at the club could be addressed. Flagging membership was the main issue, and the club's dress code needed to be elevated to Royal standards. Commodore Augustus Nanton, whose name graces several Winnipeg and Lake of the Woods landmarks, decreed that "male members have to wear white flannels with jacket (blazer) when not sailing and white duck pants or fine khaki when sailing."

A social highlight for both Winnipeg and Kenora was the annual gala dance that occurred after the racing season was completed. The first ball — in 1928 — was a smashing success, and was attended by most of Winnipeg's monied elite. The second ball wasn't so festive. It coincided with the exact date of the 1929 stock market crash.

The Duke of Kent's 1941 visit was another high water mark. The clubhouse, docks and outbuildings received improvements that are evident today. After World War Two the club started building a nation-wide reputation in the field of competitive sailing. For nearly 30 years, highly regarded sailors, including Olympic and class champions, were based at the RLWYC.

These days the club serves more as a centre for instruction and youth sailing. Tennis is popular as well. And many of Winnipeg's elite still look forward to the annual gala party on the August long weekend, a chance to dress up and look back on another successful summer season amongst the stony islands and lapping waters of the Lake of the Woods. ■

Lake of the Woods Museum

PAM

William Van Horne, general manager of the CPR, recognized early on the importance of developing recreational facilities close to his company's railway.

Supplying, and defending the Red River Settlement thus added a new impetus to development in the Lake of the Woods region, particularly when in 1869, the government of Canada took control of the former land holdings of the Hudson's Bay Company. In 1868, construction began on the Dawson Road, which would provide an overland link between the Red River Settlement and the North West Angle. By 1872, three steam tugboats plied the route between Fort Frances and Lake of the Woods. And these same vessels enabled Wolseley to transport his cannons to the Red River to quell the insurrection.

In 1876, a new age of commerce was launched when the good ship *Speedwell* hit the lake. She was the first privately owned boat on Lake of the Woods, and at 20 tons, was an imposing sight. She lasted until 1882, when Wiley's Reef claimed her. But the day of the canoe was fading fast. Soon other commercial boats plied the lake, and as the population grew, many of the steamers were outfitted for passenger traffic. Among the first to capitalize on this expanding market were two entrepreneurs named Brydges and Lewis. Operating under the banner of the

"Pioneer Navigation Company," they ran a fleet of four steamers between Fort Frances and Rat Portage. The largest was the *Edna Brydges*, which could accommodate 60 passengers. A few decades later the trip became downright festive, when the good ship *Monarch* joined the Lake of the Woods fleet. The *Monarch* was a party boat with a 20 by 40 foot dance floor, and a three-piece band for moonlight dance cruises. The *Monarch* was a popular boat for courting couples, but passengers were cautioned that only "temperance beverages" were sold on board.

Settlement and development on the lake became downright feverish with the coming of the railway. The demand for building materials was so great that by 1890, seven lumber mills operated in the Rat Portage area. The first of these was the Keewatin Lumber and Manufacturing Company. As the construction of the CPR moved ahead at a breakneck pace, there were great opportunities to make a profit from the railway workers, all of whom had to be housed, fed, and entertained. Stores, hotels, and a post office popped up as fast as they could be nailed together. It was a bonanza, a land boom, and anyone who wanted to make fast money was moving to Rat Portage. In 1877, the white population of Rat Portage consisted of two families. Seven years later, the population had mushroomed to 720.

The stretch of track between Winnipeg and Rat Portage was completed in 1882. The completion of the railway stimulated a thriving and diverse economy. The 1890s brought a boom in mining, and from 1891 to 1895, virtually all of Ontario's gold production came from the Lake of the Woods region. Flour milling also became big news. The first flour mill was constructed near Darlington Bay, and quickly became the largest in Canada. Western wheat was shipped to Keewatin, milled, and then sent east or west as the market required. Because of the railway, the Lake of the Woods was also accessible to Winnipeggers, and they didn't wait long in coming. A steady flow of summer residents set up camps around Keewatin Beach, Coney Island, and on islands within rowing distance of Rat Portage.

Further out on the lake, miners, prospectors, and fast-buck artists harvested the lake's natural bounty. Commercial fishermen began "strip mining" sturgeon, which were found in incredible numbers in those days. A United States Museum reported that "Lake of the Woods is the greatest

The new railway connected Lake of the Woods to the monied classes of Winnipeg, who soon became the first cottagers.

CP Limited C. 1885

Whisky Smugglers
of the Lake of the Woods

BY JAKE MACDONALD

The Lake of the Woods has weathered two periods of prohibition. The first liquor ban was enacted during the 1880s, when the Canadian Pacific Railway pushed its way through Rat Portage (now Kenora). The "navvies" who worked on the railway were generally a hard-drinking bunch. Tent-camp brothels and saloons surrounded every construction camp. And after a night of carousing, the navvies didn't feel like getting up for work in the morning. So CPR management lobbied the government to declare a total ban on liquor within seven miles of the rail line. It seemed like a good theory. Without booze, the gamblers and prostitutes would have a harder time separating the railway workers from their dollars.

But liquor was still freely available on the south end of the lake. And bootleggers made a lot of money buying booze in Minnesota and hauling it up to the north end of the lake, where they would stash it in the bush. One favourite hiding place was Whisky Island, where to this day, rumours persist of forgotten whisky caches lost in the forest. Much of the smuggled liquor found its way into speakeasies that were based on islands just south of the seven-mile limit. After work, boatloads of rowdy railway workers headed south for a drink. Plowing their way back to Kenora in the middle of the night, many of them became lost in the maze of islands or overturned their boats and drowned.

Once the railway moved on, Rat Portage became Kenora, and prohibition became a memory. But Canada wasn't through with social experiments yet. Throughout the country, the Woman's Christian Temperance Union was lobbying the government to limit or prohibit the sale of alcohol. And the Union had a very active chapter in Kenora. During the Great War, prohibitionists made significant progress with lawmakers. And on the morning of March 13, 1918, *The Kenora Miner and News* delivered a shocking announcement — CANADA WILL BE VERY VERY DRY. Spurred on by this news, the rough-and-ready denizens of Kenora began stocking up for their long drought. Retail sales at local liquor outlets went into overdrive and exporters shipped thousands of gallons of booze to Manitoba.

Prohibition became law on April Fool's Day and was soon followed by a booming trade in home-distilled liquor. The laws could be circumvented in a number of ways. Many people built their own home distilleries. And others obtained a doctor's prescription and kept their bars stocked with booze that was labeled "strictly for medicinal purposes." With so many people ignoring the law, the Ontario government finally canceled prohibition in 1927.

But the United States stubbornly persisted with prohibition and the disparity in laws opened up a huge smuggling industry on Lake of the Woods. Late at night cottagers would be awakened by the thundering passage of speedboats running booze down to the States. And according to local legend, even Al Capone got into the act, with a custom-fitted boat that he regularly sent up to Kenora. In 1933, the United States finally gave up on the prohibition experiment. But it was a profitable period for lawbreakers. Police estimated that in the years between 1927 and 1933, over one million gallons of liquor were smuggled to the United States. ▪

sturgeon pond in the world." In 1895, fishermen hauled 1,643,072 pounds of this gentle giant out of the lake. Ten years later, the catch had fallen to 50,000 pounds. When the sturgeon were wiped out, fishermen turned to whitefish, pickerel, and pike. For many years, the Lake supported a thriving commercial fishery. But as the tourist industry developed, commercial fishing was seen as incompatible with sports fishing, and commercial licences were phased out.

Along with hard-drinking railway workers, and ladies of the night, Rat Portage also had its share of political scandals. In 1904, the settlement was renamed Kenora. ("Ke" for Keewatin, "Nor" for Norman, and "Ra" for Rat Portage) and nobody seemed to know which province the new town belonged to. Manitoba claimed everything west of what is now Thunder Bay, but Ontario begged to differ. The feds sided with Manitoba, and appointed a commission to examine the dispute. To everyone's surprise, the commission ruled in favour of Ontario. The Dominion government refused to accept the ruling, and even went so far as to pass an act in parliament establishing Manitoba's claim. Ontario simply ignored this act, and for two years Kenora had two

provincial governments. Both provinces tried to collect revenue from town residents, and each province had their own police force.

This comedy reached its peak in 1883, when the residents were allowed to vote for members in both provincial legislatures. In a fit of pique, the two police forces began arresting each other. And while the cops squabbled, the sinners flourished. Taverns overflowed with good cheer, and prostitutes took over the streetcorners. Railway

officials tried to ban both activities, claiming that their workers were too hung-over to show up for work. But in response to the ban, enterprising proprietors simply moved out onto the lake and set up shop on various islands. Finally, the townsfolk rebelled against the chaos, and formally requested to be part of Ontario. Even with that, the matter had to be resolved by the Privy Council in England.

To service the new cottage class, a thriving marina developed on Kenora's waterfront.

THE NEW STEEL STEAMER
'Keenora'
(CAPT. A. THOMPSON)
Class A 1 at Lloyd's
Will Sail on Saturday,
May 7, at 7 p.m. and
hereafter sail regular y
on WEDNESDAY
and SATURDAY for FORT FRANGES, KOOCHICHING and Intermediate Points,
connecting with steamers for Mine Centre, Seine City, Bell City, and Rainy Lake City,
Comforts for Passengers unsurpassed—Freight handled carefully and with despat h—Consign
ou goods an I travel by the Keenora—For freight and passenger rates apply to
MARGETSON & CO., Opp. Imp. Tank, Town Agts. WALTER ROSS, Rat Portage.

As a comedy of errors, the boundary dispute was rivaled only by the international border fiasco, which took nearly 150 years to resolve. Briefly stated, the trouble began when the Treaty of Paris, (which ended the American Revolutionary War) was being negotiated in 1783. Clearly, a boundary had to be established between the two countries. Unfortunately, the men in powdered wigs had only rudimentary maps of the fur traders for reference material. So they proposed that the border follow the Rainy River "to the Lake of the Woods, thence through the said lake to the most northwestern part thereof, and from thence on a due west course to the river Mississippi."

This seemed workable, except for one detail — a line drawn "due west" from the lake would fail to contact the Mississippi River, because the river lies south of Lake of the Woods. So they went back to the drawing board. An international commission was reformed, and it ruled that the first step was to establish the most northwestern part of the lake. Surveyors were duly engaged, and off they went. After stumbling around for some time in the labyrinth of bays and blind channels, they threw up their hands, and said it was impossible. Enter Dr. I.L. Starks, astronomer. After much exploration, he likewise threw in the towel. Studying a reasonably accurate map of the lake, he laid a ruler on it at an exact NE to SW direction. He then moved the ruler left, and the last point of land it touched was the long sought after "most northwestern point." A line was then dropped due south to the 49th parallel, and the border was established. No doubt sick of the whole issue, both sides cried uncle. Apparently, the Americans didn't care that this line of demarcation left a small portion off Minnesota inaccessible by land from the United States, where it remains so today.

Lake of the Woods Museum

The *Keenora* plied the waterways of Lake of The Woods for 20 years before being dismantled and shipped for a new nautical career on Lake Winnipeg in 1918.

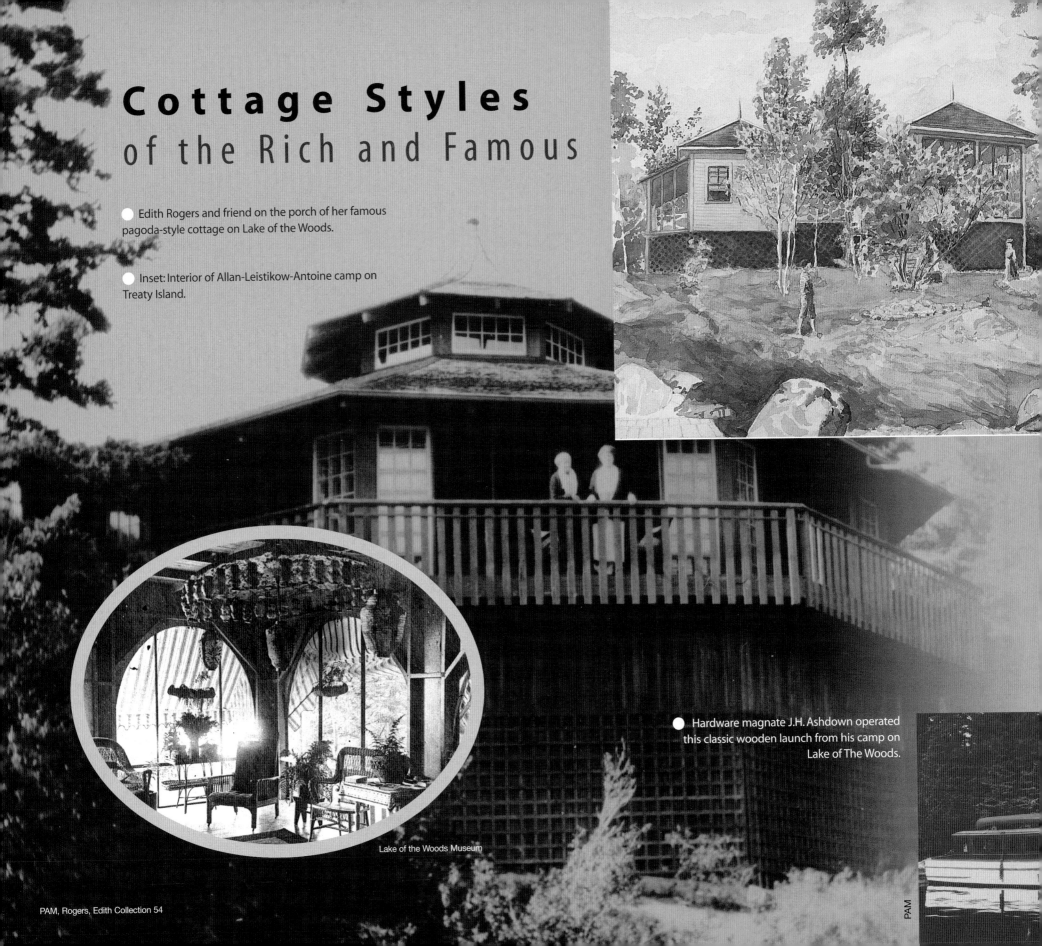

Cottage Styles
of the Rich and Famous

● Edith Rogers and friend on the porch of her famous pagoda-style cottage on Lake of the Woods.

● Inset: Interior of Allan-Leistikow-Antoine camp on Treaty Island.

● Hardware magnate J.H. Ashdown operated this classic wooden launch from his camp on Lake of The Woods.

Lake of the Woods Museum

PAM, Rogers, Edith Collection 54

PAM

● Left: Businessman Frederick Phillipps did this watercolour of his cottage, circa 1900.

● Right and Below: Two examples of today's millionaire cottages.

Tom Thomson

Lake of the Woods' cottagers utilized every type of boat transportation from canoes to sailboats to large wooden launches.

HAVING RAPIDLY GROWN from an isolated fur trading post to a bustling boom town in a relatively short time, Kenora now faced an uncertain future. The lumber industry was dealt a severe blow by the construction of a railway along the south shore of the lake. This new transportation link with western Canada fostered stiff competition, and Kenora's saw mill industry declined steadily. To compound matters, by 1905, commercial fishermen had depleted the lake, and mining had all but vanished. This downturn was somewhat mitigated by the coming of the pulp industry. The mill, which was completed in the 1920s remains the largest single employer in the Kenora area. But something more important was about to happen.

Lake of the Woods was (and is) wildly beautiful. It soon became the place for wealthy

Even early cottagers sometimes gave in to the temptation of attaining an all-over tan.

Lake of the Woods Museum

The Romance of the
Grace Anne II

BY JAKE MACDONALD

Above: Grace Anne Macdonald Forlong and her husband, John Forlong.

Below: Loading the hull of the Grace Anne II onto a railway flatbed car.

Lake of the Woods Museum

It was the 1920s, and the Lake of the Woods was on a roll. Local entrepreneurs were making money from gold and timber, and affluent city people were building palatial cottages all over the lake. Heiress Grace Anne Macdonald Forlong and her husband, John Forlong, loved boats; they loved entertaining friends and they loved each other. So in 1930, John seized upon an idea that would satisfy all three passions. Consulting with the legendary boatbuilder Herb Ditchburn, he ordered a secret birthday present for his wife — a luxurious 85-foot wooden yacht.

The Ditchburn family of Gravenhurst, Ontario got started building boats back in England, during the days of the Spanish Armada. Eventually the Ditchburns emigrated to the New World, and continued building boats for wealthy clients in the Muskoka Lakes district of Ontario. Oil barons, brewery magnates, and General Motors presidents were among the many proud owners of Ditchburn boats, and John Forlong wanted a boat that would stand out from all the rest. Working at their customary scrupulous pace, the Ditchburn artisans spent four months building the masterpiece. The finished yacht (built to replace an earlier, smaller Forlong boat) was named "Grace Anne II."

Herb Ditchburn had a lot riding on this project. He didn't have John Forlong's deep pockets, and the Depression had put a damper on the luxury boat market. When the gleaming, flag-bedecked *Grace Anne II* slid down the ramp into Lake Simcoe, the crowd of onlookers and boat builders had no inkling that they were giving a standing ovation to the Ditchburn Boatbuilding Company's last boat. The *Grace Anne* had helped drive the company into bankruptcy.

Despite his financial problems, Herb Ditchburn was determined to finish the *Grace Anne* with style. A daunting task still lay ahead — delivering the immense yacht across the Canadian Shield to the Lake of the Woods. From Orillia, the *Grace Anne* motored down the Trent-Severn Waterway to Georgian Bay, and from there it crossed the treacherous waters of Lake Huron and Lake Superior to Port Arthur — a trip of almost 2,000 kilometers.

Now came the hard part. In Port Arthur, Herb Ditchburn supervised the temporary dismantling of the boat. The superstructure was taken off and the engine removed, then the hull was lifted onto a railway car. The 100-ton boat was too wide for the railway line, so it was tilted up on its side and fastened in a cradle. Engineers from the Ditchburn plant and officers of the CNR then carefully measured each and every trestle, bridge, overpass and rock cut on the railway line. It looked tight, so they built a small scale model of the rail line, and maneuvered a tiny model of the *Grace Anne* through the narrow spots. Their preparations paid off, but just barely. On delivery day, the yacht headed west at 60 miles per hour. At CNR bridge #681 near Fort Frances it whistled through the steel trestlework with just two inches to spare.

In the town of Kenora, *The Miner and News* was having a hard time keeping quiet about the birthday surprise. While Mrs. Forlong stayed out at the cottage, playing dumb, the newspaper gave daily updates. "Forlong Yacht Expected Soon on Lake Waters," one headline announced. "Forlong Yacht to Arrive Here Few Days Time." When the boat finally arrived it was presented to the lady, then whisked off to a cavernous new boathouse

● Built in 1930, the *Grace Anne II* still graces the waterways of Lake of the Woods.

on Coney Island, where it was inspected for damage and carefully fitted out with luxurious furnishings and hardware. Typically, Herb Ditchburn had done a first-class delivery job. Although the *Grace Anne* is a particularly long and narrow craft, with considerable potential for flexion amidships, there wasn't a stress fracture in the hull or even a hairline crack in the white paint.

Over the next 15 years the *Grace Anne II* cruised the lake under the stewardship of the Forlong family. Then in 1946, she was sold to Ralph Erwin, the owner of the Salisbury House restaurant chain. Under Erwin's ownership, the boat operated as a floating hunting and fishing lodge. A dozen sportsmen could charter the boat for a week for $2,500, play cards and smoke stogies to their heart's content. The experience was marketed to American anglers, and featured "Experienced Guides and Grand Canadian Style Meals." This marketing formula didn't work particularly well, and over the next few years the *Grace Anne* went through a number of personal makeovers. Like her neighbour to the north — Minaki Lodge — *Grace Anne* hailed from a bygone era. And until the 3M Company bought her in 1954, it wasn't clear whether anyone was willing to maintain her in the plush style to which she was accustomed.

The 3M company understood the boat, and for the next 40 years they spent a small fortune maintaining her. Her navigational equipment was upgraded. Her woodwork was restored to its former glory. And in the winter, she slumbered in a huge insulated boathouse with bubble pumps that prevented ice from forming. In 1994, the captain of the *Grace Anne*, along with several other former employees, purchased her from 3M. And today she cruises the Lake of the Woods as a first-class floating resort. The boat is still a stirring sight, and stands as an enduring tribute to the craftsmen who built her. She tends to appear without notice, parading through some narrow cut between the islands. And when she glides past with her flags snapping in the wind, she seems to inspire a moment of pure nostalgia in onlookers. Adults drop what they're doing, dogs bark, and children wave madly at the passing queen of the lake. ■

Winnipeggers to build summer cottages — to escape the oppressive heat of the city. One of the first to build was Alexander Macdonald, a prominent wholesale grocer. He built on Coney Island in 1889, and a few years later many of the wealthy grain merchants, led by the Richardson family, followed his example. Lavish cottages or "camps" were the norm, as evidenced by the property of William Allan, scion of the Allan Steamship Line. Built in 1906, the cottage featured 22 bedrooms, and was reputed to have hosted such luminaries as John Wayne, Jimmy Cagney and James Stewart. As motor boats became more reliable, and thus more prevalent, huge boathouses began to proliferate. Many of these properties are still in use, and are preserved despite the cost of maintaining century-old wooden structures.

Early transportation between the mainland and the island cottages was by livery, or what is called today, water taxi. Private boats soon eliminated the need for this service, and the Lake of the Woods became home to some of the largest private vessels on inland waters. Many highly skilled artisans from the eastern ship building trade emigrated to Rat Portage, where their skills

ONTARIO WELCOMES YOU

H.Kaplarcik-Foreman.
Ed.Heinz-Foreman.
J.Hertz-Foreman.
H.C.Nixon-Div. Eng'r.
Jno.D.Baby-Asst.Dist.Eng'r.

H.Herbacz-Foreman.
S.I.Gislason-Draftsman.
H.Cairns-Chief Mechanic.
R.Smith-Road Inspector.
R.T.Lyons-Dist.Eng'r.

Engineering and Construction Staff.

TRANS-CANADA HIGHWAY
Kenora-Manitoba Section
1932

C.G.Linde

Lake of the Woods Museum

● Manitobans flocked to the Lake of the Woods area in ever-increasing numbers when a road connection to Winnipeg was finally completed in 1932.

were in great demand. The most famous of these was J.W. Stone. Stone was one of the first builders to concentrate on building private pleasure craft. His crowning achievement was the *Minniwawa*, built for a Winnipeg grain merchant. Launched in 1930, the *Minniwawa* was 79 feet long, and set the standard for quality and opulence. In recent times, there has been a revival of interest in vintage wooden boats, and the lake now features a growing number of beautifully restored craft.

Fish have always been one of the main resources around the Lake of the Woods country. And today, the statue of "Husky the Musky" beside the main highway into Kenora testifies to the mythic importance of angling in local culture. The lake here has dozens of plush resorts that were built for no other reason than fishing. Down around Sioux Narrows, on the east shore of the Lake of the Woods, the deep, cold waters make a unique habitat for lake trout. On the west side of the lake, the shallow fertile bays bordering Manitoba produce huge schools of walleye (which Manitobans tend to call "pickerel"). The north end of the lake, around Kenora, has lots of rock rubble,

● Though somewhat depleted by over-fishing, the
Lake of the Woods still provides excellent opportunities
to catch walleye, northern pike, bass, lake trout and even
the elusive muskie.

Tom Thomson

The Water Trick

BY CHARLES GORDON

It is a huge lake and it is many different lakes to the thousands of people who are on it. Amazingly enough, they all call it the same thing — The Lake.

Lake of the Woods is a social lake to many people. They golf at the Kenora Golf and Country Club, dine at the Yacht Club, go back and forth, their kids hang out together, taking lessons of various sorts.

But the Lake is an anti-social lake to others. They come down (never up, from no matter which direction) and immediately hide themselves away from all but their families. They hang out on their islands, taking the boat into the Safeway dock or the laundromat when absolutely necessary, but otherwise leaving the socializing to other people.

There is an inner lake, a congested scene near Town, as Kenora is called, with fast boats and jet skis showing off for each other.

There is an outer lake, stretching many miles to the south and east, where the boat traffic is light, the automobile is a distant memory, the water is clear and the pelicans glide through the sunset.

It is all The Lake.

There is the sporty lake, host to international bass tournaments and a regatta that draws sailors from all over the continent.

There is the contemplative lake, from which a sleepy eye is cocked at the bass boats buzzing across the bay, the sailboats looming on the other side of the channel, the eye then returning to a mystery book, then closing for a stolen half hour or two.

There is the commuter's lake, target of a ritual dash down the Trans-Canada on a Friday evening, the adjustment from office to hammock quickly made, then just as quickly reversed two days later.

There is the long-timer's lake, where the wristwatch is taken off and not put back on for three weeks or a month, the city clothes stuffed at the back of the closet, the books piled beside the bedside table, the mail unforwarded.

It is many different lakes and one Lake. What all the lakes have in common is an unmatched physical beauty, a dramatic tendency in the weather and a psychological separation from the city. The Lake, unlike other lakes closer to the population centres of Ontario, is not a suburb with water. Despite its proximity to Winnipeg, it does not take on the

The Rev. Charles W. Gordon, also known as the best-selling author Ralph Connor, shares a tender moment with his wife at the cottage.

personality of the city. Its own personality is too strong for that, always has been.

At our lake, the one my family has known since about the turn of the twentieth century, we are all kinds of people, but the lake forces us to drop our city identities at the dock. Among the occupations represented in my generation, the third of five to have inhabited the island, are writer, editor, university professor, choreographer, executive, teacher, clergyman, social worker and civil servant. All of us feel as if we do important work in the days that they are not at the Lake. At the lake, that work is dismissed quickly.

"How was your year?" someone will ask.

"Oh, it was fine," will be the reply, and discussion will quickly turn to the corner of the dock that seems to be sagging or the prospects of the wood stove lasting another summer or the funny thing somebody said during the rummy game last night.

I suspect it is that way at most people's lake. The Lake forces you to abandon your city self and pay attention. There is a sunset, a storm, an eagle, a bear, a wind, a certain play of light. Everything else seems suddenly small.

Our Lake, the one my family has known since the turn of the century, is a combination of many of these lakes. The island where as many as 25 of us may turn up on a long weekend, is far enough from Town to be out of the jet ski stream, but not remote, by Lake standards. We are not socializers. We fish unprofessionally. Some of us commute, some of us come from farther away and stay longer.

Lake status is different from city status. Money doesn't matter, nor does fame. What matters is how we perform on the island. Performing means working on the woodpile or in the woods or in the kitchen. It means handling a canoe and being good with children. It means laughing, at yourself as well as others. It means not complaining.

It means, in the words of my late uncle, Ron Cox, being "a good camper."

When my father and his six sisters were growing up on the island, a number of important and famous people visited it to see my grandfather, who was both the minister Charles W. Gordon and the best-selling author, Ralph Connor. The main house, which now needs constant repair, was then grand. The tennis court, which is now a patch of sandy dirt with a badminton net on it, was then a tennis court with a surface of boards.

But when the stories of those visitors were told in subsequent years by the members of the second generation, they were always about the way those important visitors fitted in, how they got along with us, how suited they were to the Lake. This one was stung by a bee. This one rambled on when saying grace. This one made a scene during the rummy game. This one got lost in the canoe. This one got mad at the "Water Trick."

The "Water Trick" was a joke of my grandfather's devising. It involved the discreet pouring of a glass of water into a trough made by rolling up the part of the oilcloth that hung below the edge of the table. Those who were in on the trick would roll up the oilcloth in front of them and the stream of water would proceed down the trough, finally falling into the lap of the one person, often an important guest, who didn't know what was going on.

What a test that was for the guest — sitting there, or probably standing now, with a wet lap and 20 Gordons around the table laughing at him. Was he a good camper? Could he laugh, while quietly

The Gordon family boathouse circa 1930.

plotting revenge? (Revenge was permissible.) Or would he get angry and stomp from the room? At the Lake, the reputation of people, no matter how prominent, is measured in those moments.

To be fair, it is also measured in moments less cruel. A particular point of land is named for a person, now gone, who loved it. A path is connected with a person, now gone, who loved to walk it. A dock recalls a visitor who helped to build it. The picture of a fish, painted in oil on the back wall by my father, commemorates the visitor who caught it, 30 years ago.

It's what you do on the island that counts. That makes it a perfect refuge. Some day city work will come to it, with cell phones and computers — for the moment, it lacks electricity — but it will still be the quality of our laughter that matters most. ∎

What can you say? At the age of twelve, this boy has landed a master angler tiger muskie.

Tom Thomson

which is great crayfish habitat, which in turn makes excellent habitat for smallmouth bass. So the Lake of the Woods is not just one fishery but many.

The Winnipeg River, which runs out of the north end of the Lake of the Woods, provided early anglers with boat access to The Dalles rapids, Minaki, and Big Sand Lake. And photographs from those early days demonstrate how extraordinary the fishing must have been. In 1947, an American tourist in Minaki caught a 65 pound world record muskellunge (which was disallowed because it was caught three days before the season opened), and for years, rumours of legendary, giant muskies have persisted. Eyewitnesses invariably report that these lake monsters carry shreds of broken fishing line trailing from their jaws, and it's always possible that at least a couple of tall tales about "the one that got away" might actually be true.

The fishing camps in the Lake of the Woods region were also unique meeting places for different cultures. The guests, who were usually Americans, found themselves in close company for days at a time with local guides, who were often local Ojibways. This created an interesting

The Many Lives
of Minaki Lodge

BY JAKE MACDONALD

● This artist's rendition of the original Minaki Lodge shows its dominant position
on the Winnipeg River leading into Gun Lake before the tragic fire of 1925.

If Kubla Khan ever built himself a cottage in northern Ontario, it might have wound up looking a lot like Minaki Lodge. The second largest log building in the world, Minaki Lodge rises above the Winnipeg River like a pipe dream. It's deserted now, boarded up and closed, but the abandoned machinery, the knee-high grass on the golf course, and the deep gullies cutting through the sandy walkways only make the place seem more mythical.

On a gloomy night, with drizzle falling on the river, you can walk around the once-teeming grounds of the Lodge without seeing a living soul. On the palatial front verandah, you can gaze into the Grand Rotunda, with its moose and caribou heads, enormous stone fireplace, and hand-crafted logwork, and marvel that it's actually uninhabited. If you close your eyes for a moment, you can almost hear the ghosts — the murmur of conversation, laughter, and the lilt of a string quartet from the dining room.

For decades now, more times than is worth recounting, Minaki Lodge has been opened, closed, and put up for sale. Countless entrepreneurs have tried to turn it into a money-making operation and failed. But it should be remembered, that Minaki Lodge was never really intended to make money. It was intended to make a grand statement. Minaki Lodge was founded in the 1920s, when both the CPR and the CNR were building huge hotels along their lines, palatial inns like the Banff Springs, the Chateau Laurier, and Pictou Lodge. These hotels were supposedly built to attract passenger and tourist traffic. But in Canada, there was never much money in hauling passengers. Even in the 1920s, there was more profit in moving a keg of nails than someone's Aunt Betty. Still, the CNR had a perfectly good reason for spending a fortune on a resort hotel.

In those days, most rail freight consisted of manufactured goods from Europe. To secure contracts to move those goods across Canada, the CNR was in dire competition with the CPR. The president of the CNR, Sir Henry Thornton, believed in the powers of gentle persuasion. European magnates who did business with Henry were treated to cross-country tours of Canada, in luxury coaches, with the stupendous scenery thrown in for free. They needed places to stop along the way, so in 1924, Sir Henry decided to build a resort that would do credit to the growing image of the CNR. The so-called Minaki Inn was rebuilt from top to bottom, and a 9-hole golf course was blasted out of the forest. To create an upholstered landscape for the fairways, Sir Henry bought a farm in Dugald, Manitoba, stripped off all the topsoil, and shipped 3,000 boxcars of earth to Minaki. Everyone thought that Sir Henry had lost his mind, but the finished project put the CPR to shame. In the first week of June 1925, work crews put the finishing touches on the grand hotel. On the morning of June 11th, one day before it opened, a worker accidentally spilled a gallon of linseed oil amongst a pile of wicker furniture. The oil caught fire and the entire Lodge burned to the ground.

Undeterred, Sir Henry started over again. This time, he commissioned a whole new design for the hotel, and imported the skilled stonemasons and log builders who'd built Jasper Park Lodge, the CNR resort in Alberta. The loss of the first building was a terrible blow, but it also provided a unique opportunity for client, architect, and contractors to get it right this time around. The new Minaki Lodge, completed in 1927, was a masterpiece, massive and airy at the same time. Sunlight poured down through the stained-glass windows and illuminated the brawny granite of the walls. In the Grand Rotunda, uncluttered by support posts, the cathedral ceiling soared to a high apex of interlaced timbers. Critics of the day described it as "the finest log structure in the world."

Minaki Lodge soon became one of the most prestigious resorts in the Canadian wilderness. Throughout the '30s and the '40s the Lodge was the ideal place to go for those who wanted to fish, golf, listen to a live orchestra, honeymoon with a new wife, or any combination of the above. But in the 1950s, a road was pushed into Minaki — eliminating the railway's monopoly on travel — and more bad news arrived soon after. The whole tourist industry was changing. Now the Americans that flooded into the Canadian backwoods every summer tended to be less affluent. Most of them actually worked for a living. They were electricians and plumbers and insurance salesmen, who certainly appreciated 60-foot ceilings and immense stone fireplaces, but ultimately preferred to stay in some, unpretentious, pork-and-beans fishing camp where the fish were twice as large and the bill half as big. In 1955, the CNR sold Minaki to a private firm, who ran it into the ground, and ultimately ownership of the Lodge reverted to the Province of Ontario, bad debts and all.

The Province of Ontario spent somewhere between $30 and $50 million upgrading the Lodge — rebuilding the highway, winterizing the buildings, and adding a huge poured-concrete structure that was supposed to be a guest wing but looked like a parking garage. Auctioned off to a succession of famous suitors, including Radisson and Four Seasons, the Lodge was still unable to generate a profit. And eventually the Queen of the North was buckled down, boarded up, and put to sleep. So that's where she lies today, waiting for a prince to come. But from the look of her rotted decks and weedy golf course, her time may be finally running out. ■

Minaki's first lodge, Holst Point, burned down in 1985.

PAM, Minaki Lodge 8

arrangement in which the guest, who was often a wealthy businessman or professional, found himself subservient to a man who knew much more about the environment, boat handling, weather, and fish wilderness survival than he did. This reversal of the pecking order created unique partnership opportunities for both sides. And native guides like George Kelly, Marcel Pahpasay and Joe Loon often became life-long friends with a whole range of wealthy guests, many of whom looked forward to their one-week fishing trip to Canada as a rare opportunity to learn about the outdoors from a true master.

As the popularity of Lake of the Woods grew, and the coming of roads made the area more accessible, the outlying lakes began to develop cottage communities. The village of Minaki, approximately 40 kilometers north of Kenora, got an enormous shot in the arm when the CNR ran its mainline through the village in 1911. A colourful character named Skipper Holst built a lodge at the intersection of Gun Lake and the Winnipeg River. And the CNR, in an attempt to lure business away from its rival railway to the south, built an enormous log castle called Minaki

● Jake MacDonald's home away from home — a floating cottage near Minaki.

Tom Thomson

A gentle breeze, a gin and tonic, and a sunset like you would never see back in the city.

Lodge. At that time, there were only two possible routes into Minaki, by railway or by boat from Kenora. It was a lot of work getting downriver from Kenora, and even more work getting back. The Dalles Rapids were fast enough to overpower any but the strongest outboard motors, and it was easy to get lost in the maze of islands and channels. But Minaki appealed to nonconformists and innovators — cottagers who weren't much interested in the polite and wealthy cottage community growing up around Kenora.

Being less trendy than Lake of the Woods, Minaki, along with Black Sturgeon, Pelican Pouch, Ena Lake, Laclu and other smaller cottage communities, developed a sort of counter-culture, in which the cottage was seen as less of a status symbol, and more of an opportunity to live in close, rustic contact with nature. In many cases, these new owners built their own cottages, and took great pride in the result, no matter how crude. This ethic of self-reliance is still very much evident in those outlying cottage communities today. Instead of hiring local contractors, those cottagers tend to tackle the basic cottage chores

In Their Own Words: Minaki

BY GORD LAIDLAW (AS TOLD TO DOUGLAS ALLEN)

Gord and Betty preparing a shore lunch at Minaki, circa 1944.

Gord Laidlaw is the former president of National Testing Laboratories. He and his wife Betty live in Minaki, Ontario from May to October, and the rest of the year in Winnipeg.

"Dad had heard that there was land available in Minaki, so he and two friends went out in the summer of 1910. The Grand Trunk railway wasn't finished yet, so they had to take the old steamer up from Kenora. I think it was called the Kathleen. In those days, all you had to do was have the land surveyed, pay a small registration fee, and it was yours.

None of them had any carpentry experience, but they were determined to build their own cottages, and over the next few years they erected some rough shacks. I'm still repairing them!

By the time the family started coming down, the railway was complete. Mother would order the groceries from Eaton's, and we'd all get on the train. When we got to Minaki, everything was loaded into Giroux's launch, and out we'd go to the cottage. For water, we'd take a big pail, a dipper, and a dish cloth down to the shore. We'd cover the pail with the dish towel as a filter, and ladle the water in. Of course, we had a cook stove, so cutting wood was a never-ending chore. Dad cut a trap door in the floor, and poured some concrete, and that was our ice container.

Dad was a teacher, so we went to the cottage at the end of the school year, and stayed for the whole summer. Usually Dad had to go back to the city for two weeks, and Mother and the kids would stay. We were taught to amuse ourselves, and to make do with what we had, and that's the way I raised my kids. As a boy, when I went fishing, I'd put some old brown paper on a straight hook, and troll it out the back of the canoe on some string. It worked just fine. The people that grew up that way love the place and forever want to come back. Those who had all the toys and amusements got sick of it and never came back.

We always had a canoe, and a row boat, and eventually Dad got a Peterborough with an old Muncie four horse on the back. It didn't start very well, but once it did it was very reliable. But you had to watch, because at that time the water was much lower than it is now. We had two rocks in front of our place. One we called Elbe, and the other St. Helena. That was because if you hit them, one you could get off, and the other you couldn't.

Betty and I got married in 1943, and we had our wedding night at the old Minaki Inn. Then we went out to the cottage for the rest of our honeymoon. I had a very hectic business, and had to work every Saturday until noon. Then I'd get on the *Flyer*, which took about 5 hours to get to Minaki. Betty would pack three kids into the boat, and drive into town to get me. Then it would be back on the train on Sunday night at seven. Speaking of the train, in1947 we were having our house in Winnipeg built, and we closed the cottage a week before Labour Day. Because of that we missed the [Dugald] train wreck. We would almost certainly have been killed because we always sat in the front coach.

After I retired, Betty and I would come down shortly after ice-out, and stay until Thanksgiving weekend. We travelled, but we never planned any trips that interfered with our time in Minaki. When I was a bit younger, my son-in-law and I would ski out to the cottage in the winter. Never could get the floor warm, but the bunks were always toasty.

We've deliberately kept our place rustic. We don't have hydro, there's no phone, no television, no hot-tub, and we wouldn't have it any other way. Looking back I'm eternally grateful to my Dad for introducing me to Minaki, all the best that life has to offer is right outside the porch." ∎

Gord Laidlaw has never allowed polio to slow him down.

Perhaps nothing defines northern lake country more than the beautiful plumage and mournful sound of the loon.

Tom Thomson

themselves, and many a college-educated professional has acquired a brand-new respect for plumbers and carpenters in the process. On Lake of the Woods, cottagers might take pride in their powerful ski boats and eight-person Jacuzzis. But in Minaki, they tend to boast about the fact that they still use kerosene lamps.

Attracted to the latter point of view, I eventually settled in Minaki myself. But I'd be less than honest if I didn't admit to an occasional passing fascination with the idea of building a helicopter pad on the roof of my float house. Like most cottagers, however, I've found that my big ideas have had to be balanced against other considerations – making a living, for example. So if I can squeeze in four or five weeks at the lake, every season, I feel like I've turned in an acceptable performance. Like most cottagers, I maintain a deep, almost fanatical devotion to my place on the water. And like most cottagers, I've found it important to break away from the cottage that my parents built on Laclu and establish a summer place of my own.

My mother and my siblings still gather at the old cottage at Laclu, and sometimes on the way to or from Minaki I'll swing by to visit them. My dad, having been crippled by a stroke, doesn't get to the cottage anymore. But the place still shows the evidence of his dreams and handiwork.

As I mentioned earlier, the site was once a dairy farm — a huge hayfield. So my father planted a hundred trees on the property — spruce, maple, ash, and crabapple. And in each scrawny tree, he installed a home-made birdhouse. Today, those spindly saplings have grown up into a lush forest. And those old birdhouses shelter a remarkable variety of birds — flickers, warblers, wrens, swallows, jays, and song sparrows. On any summer day, the bird chatter is so intense that, as you're hiking down the hill to the cottage, it's like walking through a leafy, sun-dappled New Orleans Jazz Festival of birds. Someday, my parents' kids — like other cottage kids from Clear Lake to Lake of the Woods — will have to sort out what's going to become of the old place. But no matter what decision we make, this place, this dream, will always belong to them. ∎

Tom Thomson

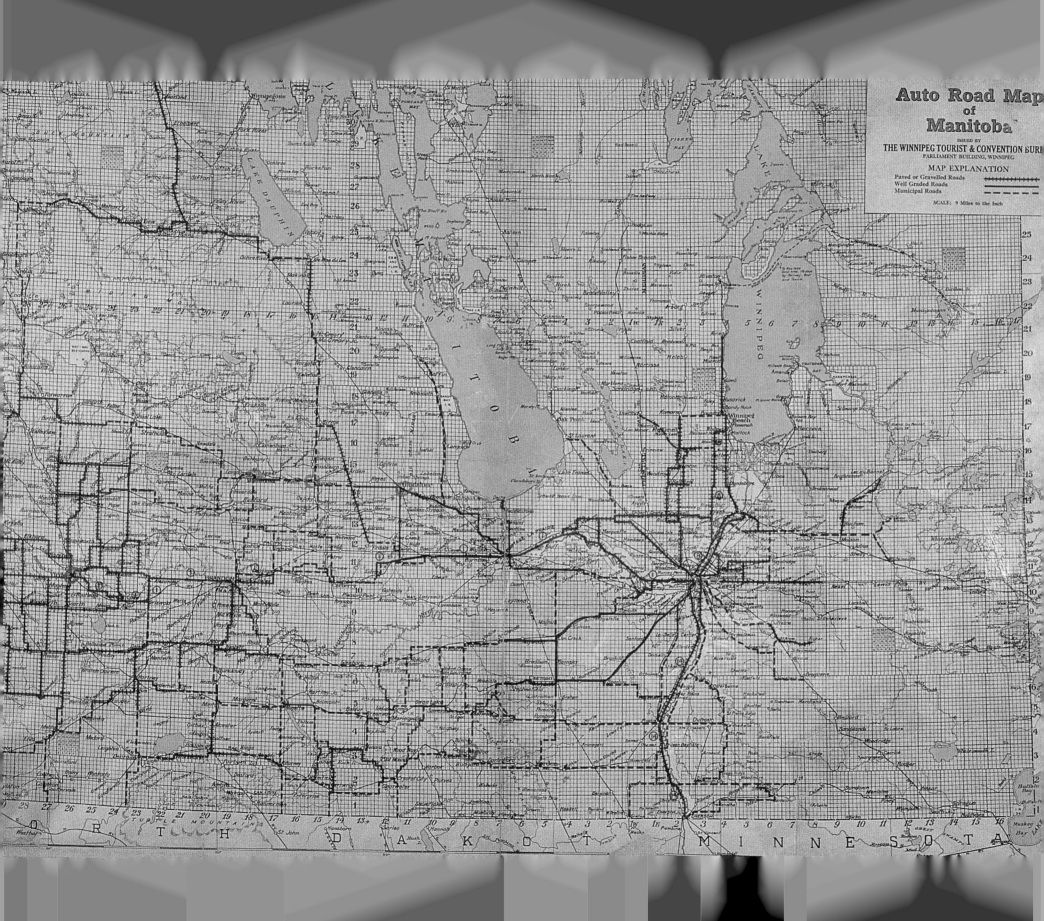

Auto Road Map of Manitoba — Issued by The Winnipeg Tourist & Convention Bureau, Parliament Building, Winnipeg

MAP EXPLANATION
Paved or Gravelled Roads
Well Graded Roads
Municipal Roads

SCALE: 9 Miles to the Inch

ACKNOWLEDGMENTS

The editors would like to thank the following people and organizations
for their assistance in preparing this book:

Lori Nelson, The Lake of the Woods Museum; Elizabeth Blight, Public Archives of Manitoba;
David Friesen, Friesens Corp.; Lorna Tergesen; Trevor Kennerd; Charmagne de Veer, Jewls Dengl;
Herbert Mueller; Dale Cummings; Yude Henteleff; Gord Laidlaw; Paul Vincent; and Violet Ploshynsky.